WITH HUMOUR AND HOPE

LEARNING

FROM OUR MOTHERS'

DEPRESSION

AND ALCOHOLISM

CHRISTINE PEETS

National Library of Canada Cataloguing in Publication Data

Peets, Christine, 1952-
        With humour and hope : learning from our mothers' depression and alcoholism

Includes bibliographical references.
ISBN 1-55212-964-0

        1. Depression, Mental--Prevention.   2. Alcoholism--Prevention.
3. Children of depressed persons.   4. Children of alcoholics.
I. Title.

HV5137.P44 2001   362.2'5   C2001-903054-1

TRAFFORD

On-demand publishing includes promotions, retail sales, manufacturing, order fulfilment, accounting and collecting royalties on behalf of the author.

Suite 6E, 2333 Government St., Victoria, B.C. V8T 4P4, CANADA
Phone   250-383-6864   Toll-free   1-888-232-4444 (Canada & US)
Fax   250-383-6804   E-mail   sales@trafford.com
Web site   www.trafford.com   trafford publishing is a division of trafford holdings ltd.
Trafford Catalogue #01-0366   www.trafford.com/robots/01-0366.html

10   9   8   7   6   5   4   3   2

March 2006

Sandy:

WITH HUMOUR AND HOPE:
Learning from Our Mothers'
Depression and Alcoholism

*To my husband Jim
and our sons,
Eric and Jeremy,
for their constant love and support*

*And to my mother, June Kane Dunlop,
who even after her death
is teaching me important life lessons*

*Always keep humour
and hope alive!*

Christine

TABLE OF CONTENTS

Acknowledgement . . . . *i*

Introduction . . . . *v*

Chapter One
My Story *1*

Chapter Two
Are We Doomed to Repeat the Past? *15*

Chapter Three
Some Definitions That May Help *31*

Chapter 4
Under the Influence *55*

Chapter 5
Eat, Drink and Be Merry *71*

Chapter Six
Moving Forward *87*

Research Information *109*

Appendix *115*

Epilogue *119*

Bibliography *121*

Resources *125*

Endnotes -Chapter One *12*

Endnotes -Chapter Two *28*

Endnotes -Chapter Three *51*

Endnotes -Chapter Four *68*

Endnotes -Chapter Five *83*

Endnotes -Chapter Six *107*

ACKNOWLEDGEMENTS

It was my fingers that were pressed to the keyboard to write this book, but I had a lot of people whose hands were on my shoulder guiding me, encouraging me, and hugging me through the process.

First and foremost, I must thank my husband Jim and our two sons Eric and Jeremy for their encouragement, patience, and assistance in bringing this labour of love from ideas in my head to the printed page. I'm not sure they understood my need to write this, but they supported the project along the way, and helped where and when needed. Jim suggested some editing changes. Eric designed my website and a web page for the book, and continues to provide technical support. Jeremy helped with typing much of the reference material, including the bibliography and resource list. Their unconditional love and support, and taking care of the household stuff when needed, is immeasurable.

My sister, Diane Palmer, is always there when I need her, and she came through again for me, acting as my main editor. They say you can choose your friends, but not your relatives. We are sisters by birth, and have become good friends, for which I will always be grateful.

Members of my mother's family shared both happy and sad memories of her with me, which helped to put my story into context. They have also been very supportive of this project, even though what I am writing might be painful for them to remember.

I must thank all of the women who shared their poignant, sometimes tragic, sometimes funny, stories for inclusion in this book. Their contributions made this book so much richer. They also affirmed that I was not alone in dealing with a mother's depression and alcoholism. The support and encouragement from these women, and their willing-ness to be so open about their experiences meant more to me than words could express. I have never met these women, and may never meet them, which makes their participation that much more incredible.

My sister's friend Kim Culpitt provided an email connection between Diane and me. She also provided the graphics and layout of the interior to give the book its special "look". Kim's diligence to meet very tight deadlines is a testament to her professionalism.

Nicole Denelzen, another professional graphic artist, created the front and back covers for the book, also working to meet my tight schedule. She also helped to choose the final title. Her creativity and her patience with me through the design process are appreciated. Nicole is a colleague in the Kingston & Area Home Business Association (KAHBA). She and other members of the organization have provided much needed encouragement and support of my work since I joined them in 1998.

My family doctor, Joanna McDonald, psychiatrist Zuzana Sramek, and chiropractor Marie Houde continue to provide excellent medical care. I thank them for their skill and compassion. My mother's physician spoke to me candidly about her relationship with my mother. She shared whatever information she could, without violating any confidences, about her treatment of my mother. Her help in providing context to my mother's life was most valuable. She also provided some of the information used in the chapter on defining depression and alcoholism.

Andrea O'Reilly and Ann Douglas, both published authors, gave me tremendous advice and encouragement on the research, writing, and publishing of this book. Andrea is the President of the Association for Research on Mothering (ARM). Without ARM, I would not have been connected to many of the women who shared their stories in this book. Ann is the 2001-2002 President of the Periodical Writers Association of Canada (PWAC). It is Ann's success in writing, and her sense of humour with which she writes that inspired much of the style of this book.

Sarah Campbell, Joti Bryant, and the team at Trafford Publishing provided the expertise and patience for this, my first book. I thank them for their professionalism and support.

To all of these people and many more who have encouraged this project, your love and support will always be appreciated.

Christine Peets
September 2001

INTRODUCTION

Congratulations and thank you for getting this far. I almost didn't. Writing a book is a daunting task; -- one I wasn't sure I was up to. I normally write magazine articles, but I felt there was more to say. Hence, this book.

In doing research for this book, I read many books and periodical articles on depression. That was almost enough to send me into a depression! I also read a number of books and pamphlets on alcoholism, which had me reaching for a glass of wine! You get the picture. You see, if you can look at living with these diseases with a sense of humour, there is hope that you can end them.

Whether depression and alcoholism are truly diseases may be still open to some debate. Some may call them "syndromes". For me, the debate ended long ago. When I was in the headlock of depression (my head was locked in a place that felt comfortable, but I felt truly miserable, and couldn't seem to find a way out of that misery), I did not feel well at all. I may not have been throwing up, or have any outward signs of illness. In fact, I probably looked fine, and everyone may have thought I was just weak, or being lazy. I was depressed, and it is an illness--but one for which there is a cure. I will be telling you more about my periods of depression later.

Everyone gets depressed at times. It's part of the human condition, and it probably happens to animals too. We do feel sad, angry, and lethargic from time to time. It is a normal reaction to tragic or upsetting circumstances in our lives: death, divorce, a loss or major change in paid work, the lack of paid work if we need it, or other sad events in our lives. It would likely be considered *abnormal* if we didn't get upset and depressed as a reaction to these events.

If these periods of sadness do not go away after a couple of weeks, or if they keep recurring, then you are said to be suffering from depression, and should seek help to find the root cause of the depression, and healthy ways to cope with, and end it.

As I learned, depression is sneaky, and it can be debilitating. Just when you think you're free from it, wham--you get knocked down again.

It's worse if you are already predisposed to this because your mother (or another family member) had bouts of depression. And, when you're feeling low, you might think you would feel better if you have a glass of wine, or a beer, or some other alcoholic beverage. If that works and you start to forget your troubles, you have another drink, and before you know it, you're depressed all over again. Rather than lifting your spirits-- pun intended, you're feeling depressed again, because, surprise-- alcohol is a depressant, not a stimulant. Then, you have the proverbial vicious cycle! Before you know it, the disease of alcoholism has snuck up on you. It is a progressive disease that gets worse before it gets better.

Although I learned more about depression and alcoholism from the literature, I know about it first hand. I have had periods of depression. I am obviously feeling much better-- well enough to write this book. My sister and I have also lived with, and taken care of, a depressed and alcoholic mother. If she were here, she'd deny it! In fact, for too many years, she did deny having a problem with her drinking, or anything else in her life. (Alcoholics are very good at the three "D's": denial, deception, and of course, drinking!) Sadly, Mom died in September 2000. More about her life, and death, later too. Remember that this is just the introduction.

If you are looking for a lot of medical jargon, or easy answers to ending depression and alcoholism (because you may have read a lot of other books on these subjects and not found those answers), you will have to keep looking. I do not have a medical background, nor do I understand the physiology of these diseases well enough to write about them.

As I said, I read a number of books on these subjects, many of them written by medical professionals. I have referred to many, quoted some, and listed them all in the bibliography for further reference and information. Try to read them when you're in a good mood--otherwise, you might end up depressed!

While you won't find the medical jargon, what you will find are inspirational stories from many women. They come from many walks of life, but to protect their privacy, I have only used first names. If requested, I used a pseudonym. I have not told you where they live, how old they are, or any details about their lives. I can tell you that they come from several countries, range in age from their 20s to their 50s, and have a variety of paid and unpaid work, including academics (teaching, or being a student), psychology, sociology, and anthropology.

They have all experienced depression and alcoholism. These women have looked at their lives, and their mother's lives, and found familial patterns. While trying to live healthier lives and break free of those patterns, they are trying to show their children that these patterns do not need to be repeated. They share stories of discovering ways to overcome their past, learn from their mothers' (or, in some cases, father's) depression and alcoholism, and move forward to a healthier, happier life. Those stories inspired me as I wrote this book, and I hope they will have the same impact on you. As you will read, however, talking about depression or alcoholism was not done, or is not done in many of these women's families. They find it difficult, but perhaps cathartic to talk about these illnesses, and the impact the illnesses have had on their lives, even now. I know I found writing my story difficult, but therapeutic. All of us who share our stories are all hopeful of finding ways to stop the patterns from repeating. The literature I read, and refer to, helped to put the personal stories into perspective.

I have included some charts, tables, and other information about depression and alcohol, for reference purposes. As I said, this is not a medical text, and should not be taken as such. Any information here should be confirmed with your own health professionals.

Along with the stories, there are some thoughts about the prevalence of alcohol and drugs in our society. I look at how these show up in our popular culture, and the influence that they might have on our behaviour. It is a wonder we are not all alcoholics, or depressed all of the time! I call this chapter "Under the Influence".

At the end of the book, there is a selective bibliography and selected list of resources, including websites and organizations, which you may find useful. There are some I am sure to have left out, and for that I apologize. This list gives you a place to start to find the information you need.

As you read the book, you will, I hope, gain some inspiration, and insight on healthier living. Being pre-disposed to an illness does not mean you will suffer the same fate. You just might have to work a little harder to beat the odds. Diet, exercise, medication, and therapies, both conventional and alternative, all have an impact. These are discussed in the final chapter, "Moving Forward".

In looking back on my life, and my mother's, I recognize periods of time when we both were depressed, although not likely at the same time. I have also considered carefully, how and when I use alcohol. I believe there is a pattern to it all, one that I can change. I hope I am teaching my sons how to live a healthy, happy, long life by living one myself. Writing this book is one step to that life.

In writing the book, I hope I have injected some humour into what could otherwise be a dreary subject. I don't want to make anyone more depressed than they already might be!
I may not make you laugh out loud, but I hope to at least put a smile on your face, and leave you feeling that, with humour and hope, we can learn from our past, and move forward to a better future.
Thanks for joining me on the journey.

CHAPTER ONE

My Story

CHAPTER ONE

My Story

Memories.
Light the corners of my mind.
...What's too painful to remember
We simply choose to forget.
But it's the laughter.
We will remember.
Whenever we remember.
The way we were.[i]

My mother died in September 2000 from diseases related to alcoholism and smoking. It's hard to think of her the way she was in those last years of her life. So, I try to remember better, happier times; to remember the laughter, and try to forget the tears. I am also trying to live in a healthier way by learning from my mother's unhealthy choices in her life.

I, like everyone else, store a lot of memories in the corners of my mind. I choose to forget the more painful ones. Or at least I try to forget those painful times and memories. It is not always easy, and sometimes, those painful memories can become so strong, they push everything else away.

Sometimes, it feels to me that the only relief from that pain is to withdraw from the world-- curl up on my couch, and watch television. When I have a day, or maybe even two, like that, I don't worry about it too much. If it continues, that is how I am now able to recognize that a period of depression could be starting. I don't have these episodes very often any more, but I have had them and I am always cognizant of the fact they could return.

I am only now realizing that off and on, over a period of years, I was more than depressed. It was never for any significant length of time in any given period, but I *suffered from depression* nonetheless. It depresses me to even admit that. Oh, I can justify those "couch days" any number of ways, and I have, no doubt.

Doctors helped me to justify all of the aches, pains, low moods, lack of appetite, sleep disturbances, and other "symptoms" of my illnesses. Why is it that they could never say I had a depressive disorder, and go from there?

Well, I suppose in a way, I should be glad they didn't, because if they had, I probably wouldn't be writing this book. If I had an earlier diagnosis of depression, I might not have done as much soul searching, and continue to try and understand what was wrong, why I felt so low, so often, and try so hard to feel better. I also might not have looked for others whose stories are similar to mine, and be as willing and anxious to write our stories in hopes that it will help others as well as ourselves.

I've learned that I, like many women, had my first episode of depression in my late 20s, not too long after the birth of our first child. I've learned that there is a difference between the "post- partum baby blues", and this more severe depression. I've also learned that the onset of the first episode of depression may not always be obvious, even to health professionals, so I guess I shouldn't get too upset with them for missing it. First episodes of depression are often mild and infrequent. The person who is depressed may not even know they are ill--or at least they might only think they are physically ill. Many of the symptoms are similar to having the "flu"-- headaches, upset stomachs, lethargy, and a host of other symptoms outlined in the chapter, "Some Definitions That May Help".

If you've ever cared for a baby for any length of time, you know how easy it is to fall into a routine of not taking care of yourself because you are so busy taking care of the baby. So, when the "baby blues" lead more into a state of depression, it may go unrecognized. I certainly fell into that category, not once, but twice. Our oldest son Eric was born in 1980, and my first episode of depression started about five months later. His brother Jeremy was born in 1984, and he was almost a year old when the second bout began. Although some might call this a "delayed case of the baby blues", I think it was much more serious.

It is difficult to know when a depressed mood becomes a medical condition.....When someone doesn't understand that he is in the throes of a depression, he is likely to ascribe the symptoms to erroneous causes, thereby delaying medical treatment. Not only is he confused, he also doesn't have an adequate explanation for those who are witnessing the changes, and the situation is ripe for myth, misunderstanding and distortion."[ii]

There were "mini-episodes" of depression in between those first two bouts, related to what my doctor referred to as a "hormonal, chemical imbalance in my brain". He said that it was all likely related to my PMS (pre-menstrual syndrome), and "nothing to really worry about." While the doctor was *sympathetic* to my depressed state, there was no interest in helping me find out more about the root causes of the depression.

He certainly never questioned me about a family history of depression, the way he asked about my family history of heart problems or diabetes. (He put my low moods down to being home with two young children, and not knowing very many people in the town where we lived, and prescribed a course of an anti-depressant for about six months).

He did not see the need for further treatment, or referral to a psychiatrist or psychologist. What I know now, is that without therapy to accompany the medication, that course of treatment was almost doomed to fail.

I've wondered whether I didn't press him into offering further treatment because I didn't want to be labeled as depressed. Was I being paranoid about that because, by that time, my mother was taking anti-depressants and I believed she was becoming addicted to them? She started taking that medication when she was in her 30s, supposedly to help her with occasional sleepless nights and control her blood pressure. At least that was her explanation. Although she never talked about being diagnosed with depression, and I don't believe she ever was [diagnosed], I now believe this was the start of her depression. My fear of following that pattern made me very reluctant to take any medication.

I agreed to the short course of medication for six months. That brought some relief, and I didn't want to continue to take it any longer. At times, I worried about my mood swings, but I trusted my doctor when he said there was nothing seriously wrong. I wish I had challenged him on his diagnosis. Why is it that we are so afraid to take our health care into our own hands and use the doctor as a resource, not as a leader for us to follow? I now think six months of therapy would have been more beneficial than six months of medication.

My third and most troublesome episode of depression came around 1991. This time, it went on for many months, and almost cost me my marriage. Again, both my doctor and I were fooled, by the fact that none of the low moods would last for any significant period of time. However, they were recurrent. My husband told me that "he never knew what kind of mood to expect", and that led to a lot of difficulties.

It has only been through therapy, and more careful diagnosis from the doctor I now have, that I have been able to realize that I indeed had a "mood disorder", or in simpler terms, I was suffering from depression.

Since then, I have also been diagnosed with fibromyalgia, a disease of chronic muscle fatigue, sleep disorder, and pain. Depression is one of the symptoms within the fibromyalgia syndrome, and is quite common for people with fibromyalgia to be depressed. As Dr. Frank Adams, a pain specialist from Ontario now practicing medicine in Texas[iii] said, "when you have frequent pain, and are con-stantly exhausted by the cycle of pain and muscle fatigue, it is surprising if you are *not* depressed!"

I have taken two different types of anti-depressants to help me to sleep better, thus easing the symptoms of the fibromyalgia. When the unpleasant side effects of those medications: ringing in my ears, stomach cramps, and other intestinal prob-lems were too unpleasant, I stopped taking them. I occasionally use herbal remedies such as St. John's Wort for dealing with the sleep disturbances. I have not ruled out taking another anti-depressant if I, in consultation with my doctor, felt it was necessary.

I would not, however, take the medication without going for regular therapy sessions. Fortunately, the psychiatrist I see occasionally says she would not give me medication without therapy. She believes, as do many doctors, that a combination of medica-tion and therapy is the best treatment for recurrent mild depression. Currently, I am using the therapy only route to recovery, because I am somewhat fearful of becoming dependent on medication, like my mother.

Anna Coleman wrote a piece on her surviving depression in *Complete Health Magazine*[iv] in the Spring 2001 Issue. In her article, "Riding High After Depression", she writes that there was always a "reason" for her low moods: teenage angst, college-related anxieties, postpartum depression, menstrual problems, and finally, menopause.

Did this woman invade my body? When I read that article, I thought, "She could be talking about me!" I suspect she could be talking about a lot of women.

After trying various anti-depressants, and psychiatry, Coleman came upon a more empathetic therapist. She has returned to university, and is also using yoga, meditation, and taking care of a dog to calm her moods and give her a more positive outlook on life. She writes,

"I am now able to see beautiful moments in every day, and I believe that life is a gift. The trick is to be open to each small gift as it arrives."[v]

Coleman will celebrate her 50th birthday next year, and receive her University degree as part of her celebration. She has obviously learned the trick of seeing life as a gift, to be opened slowly. What a wonderful treat!

Before I go too much further, I should give you some "biographical information". I will celebrate my 49th birthday this year. As I approach the big "5-0", I want to be healthier than I am now. I want to make sure that those painful memories stay permanently in the corners of my mind.

I don't just want to be better for me; I want to be better for my family. We all deserve as much.

Mostly, I do not want to repeat the pattern that my mother's life took after she turned 50. A short eighteen years later, she died, in a nursing home.

Her ability to take care of herself in her own home had diminished and she agreed to go to the home "until she was better". Although the nursing home staff provided excellent care, it was not what anyone had envisioned as she approached her retirement years. She died eight months after going into the nursing home. The "official" cause of death was chronic obstructive lung disease caused by excessive smoking, but depression and alcoholism were definitely contributing factors to her death, as they had caused damage to her brain, liver, and stomach.

I recently read that when you are a mother, you either become a good example or a horrible lesson to your children. My mother was both. I hope to be only the good example. American feminist, author and activist Gloria Steinem says, "the best way to teach your children how to live a unique life is to live one yourself."

It is that passion to be healthier and stronger that leads me to use different exercise programs, diets, herbal remedies, alternative therapies, and traditional medical treatments to stay healthy. Whew! I'm tired just writing all of that. No wonder I am tired of living it! I wish that eating a balanced diet, exercising a few times each week, and having a happy home life was enough.

Sadly, I know that it is not. I am lucky to have my husband, friends, and family to motivate me to keep exercising.

We are also fortunate to have a small gym run by two qualified fitness trainers, and a pool facility in our small town. My doctor says that I should consider the cost of using them as a type of retirement savings plan. I am investing in a healthier future!

Have I told you enough about me? I am no doubt telling you more than you wanted or needed to know. I always was a bit of a chatterbox. ("Christine is a bit of a chatterbox" was even written on my grade school report cards!) I thought it would be good to lay this all out, so that you know what I try to deal with. I think I'm doing a pretty good job. Hey, I'm still here, and I take myself much less seriously now than I used to. I don't "take things to heart", as my sister says, nearly as often. I laugh a lot more, at myself, and at the world.

Sometimes, though, it's just a brave face I put on for the world. Inside, I am terrified-- terrified that no matter what I do, I will become my mother. She was happy, athletic, and with a strong "support system" of friends, family and a good career as an office administrator when she was the age I am now. She lived alone, never getting into a serious relationship after she and my father divorced. In the first few years after their separation, she had a few "men-friends", but said she "enjoyed her independence too much" to let any of them develop into a real relationship. I am not laying blame, just trying to put her lifestyle choices into perspective. My mother chose to live her life, her way. She joined a ski club, played baseball, and tennis. She joined in social activities with friends from her sports clubs, and work colleagues.

Gradually though, her friends fell away as she started to drink more. In later years, she said she drank as much as she did (never thinking she drank excessively) because she spent so much time alone. Yet, she always had reasons for not wanting to join others in activities. The alcohol started to take over her life. It may have contributed to the end of her career. Later she was forced to take work that did not use her administrative skills that made her previous career so successful. The alcoholism added to what I think was the undiagnosed clinical depression that caused her to be on what became a very lonely road. I am determined not to go down that same road.

My sister and my husband will tell you that I think far too much, and analyze everything to death! I do like to think about life in general, and, my life, in particular. Somehow, by giving some thought to it, I think I can make it more ordered. Oh the things we can think, as Dr. Suess would say--or was it the scarecrow from "The Wizard of Oz"? I also like to know, or try to figure out, why things happen the way they do. At the same time, I believe that some things are fate, or destiny. I believe that while we may sometimes have no control over the things that happen, we should at least try to learn from them.

God, grant me the SERENITY
To ACCEPT the things I cannot change
The COURAGE to change the things I can
And the WISDOM to know the difference[vi]

I have that familiar prayer on a coffee mug, and write it in each new diary I begin. I am trying to accept what I cannot change, and learn from my mother's life. More importantly, I am trying to have the courage to learn from her death, and change what I can in my own life. I think that things happen for a reason, even though we may not know that reason. Before you start thinking that you are reading a book by Shirley MacLaine (whom I greatly admire, and is partially responsible for this belief in fate, and an "ordered Universe"), I am not talking about any past lives. I am definitely talking about *this* life of my mother's, and mine.

While I do occasionally drink wine, beer, and other alcohol, I worry about it sometimes. I've been told that if I *really* had a problem with alcohol, I wouldn't think about when I drink, or how much, I would just drink. There I go, analyzing things again.

The other things I analyze too much are my feelings, and my moods, both good and bad. "Just get on with life", I can hear my husband saying. He's right. I should, and I try to, just get on with it. For me, getting on with life includes looking back at depression in the past. If you don't learn from the past, you are bound to repeat the mistakes.

That's my story, or at least the first part of it. Oh no, there's more?--you are asking yourself! I'll be sharing more of my story as we go along.

Others have their stories to tell too, and I have a lot of other information to share, so, as my husband would say, "Let's get on with it."

Endnotes:

[i] Lyrics from "The Way We Were". Music by Marvin Hamlisch. Words by Alan and Marilyn Bergman. Recorded by Barbra Streisand for the movie "The Way We Were" (1973)

[ii] Papolos, Demitri F., M.D., Papalos, Janice, <u>Overcoming Depression</u> Third Edition, HarperCollins, 1997, p 9 While the Papolos' use the male pronoun, their statements are equally applicable to women.

[iii] Dr. Adams had his licence to practise medicine in Ontario revoked in 2001 after a two-year investigation into his pain therapy practices, which included prescribing types of morphine-like drugs for chronic pain. Many of his patients continue to petition the Ontario College of Physicians and Surgeons for his license to be reinstated, without conditions.

[iv] Coleman, Anna, "Riding High After Depression", <u>Complete Health Magazine</u>, Complete Health Publications, Spring 2001 Issue

[v] <u>Ibid</u>

[vi] "Serenity Prayer", also known as the "AA Prayer" as it is used by Alcoholics Anonymous and its related groups, Al-Anon and Al-Ateen. Attempts were made by checking with several people within AA and checking its website to credit the author

CHAPTER TWO

Are We Doomed To
Repeat the Past?

CHAPTER TWO

Are We Doomed to Repeat the Past?

Familial tendencies suggest a genetic transmission, but since genetic theories don't survive on hints and suggestions, intense scientific inquiry has lately been focused in this direction...Current research indicates only that the vulnerability to these disorders is 'passed down' (inherited) in families - the way a physical illness such as diabetes shows up in a family pedigree. Family studies continue to show that the relatives of people who have manic- depression or depression have a significantly higher rate of these disorders - perhaps two to three times higher - than occurs in the general population[i]

Given that we might be predisposed to depression, which we might choose to dull with alcohol, are we doomed? Will we become sad alcoholics? If so, why not just give up now and accept our fate? Because it doesn't have to be our fate! We have choices, and those choices can include living a healthier life, which might include some alcohol, and perhaps even some anti- depressant medication, but doesn't have to lead us down that path to addiction.

Elisabeth's Story:ii

My initial episode of post-natal depression, which was diagnosed by a doctor, lasted for almost a year. Another very brief episode of depression occured in 1989 when my fourth child was about 10 or 11 months old. I joined and helped run a group called PaNDA (Post and Ante- Natal Depression Association) for a couple of years. Then I had quite a severe episode of depression when my marriage was breaking up. At that stage my fifth (last) child was just about 3 or 4 months old. Over the years I have come close to further episodes of depression, but have always been able to prevent them becoming full blown. Until last year (2000) that is, when my doctor diagnosed another very serious episode of depression.

Various factors combined to cause me to become suicidal twice in one week, and to reluctantly take anti-depressants. These worked, in that they helped me over a very bad time, but I felt that if I had had more support – social, practical and emotional – I would not have needed them. I felt that they made me tolerate an intolerable situation. The symptoms of depression for me are a feeling that I am living under my own personal black cloud, severe insomnia, inability to function in daily life, agoraphobia to varying degrees, low libido, irritability, extreme sensitivity to sound, loss of appetite, exhaustion, loss of concentration. As it is only 8 months since I have come through the last episode, I would have to say that I probably do still have depressive periods. How long would I have to be free of them to be able to say that I am no longer at risk of developing depression?

I believe that my mother's depression was never diagnosed, nor even recognized. I also believe that her dependence on alcohol for a number of years is directly attributable to her depression. It is my sister (who also suffered from post-natal depression after the birth of her first child) and I who have identified my mother's depression. As far as I am aware, a doctor never diagnosed it. She may still have depressed moods, but it is hard to tell – I see her rarely, though I do talk to her on the phone almost weekly. However, her memory is beginning to fail and this is more of a worry than depression.

My mother moved to Australia from England when she was 32 (my father was 33) and she had three small children, my two brothers and myself. During the three years she lived here at that time she gave birth to my sister. She was very lonely and missed her family very much. This may have been a triggering factor. After the family returned to England my mother had two miscarriages before giving birth, after a long spell in hospital, to my youngest brother. When he was 2 we moved back to Australia again. My mother's depression seemed to be worst during the following few years. She showed various signs of depression--a lack of engagement with people other than those she <u>had</u> to see for work, school or church related events; a degree of agoraphobia. She refused to go places other than those to do with work or running the household. She developed a dependency on alcohol, and smoked all of her adult life.

Even now, Elisabeth says, her mother might find it hard to admit that she had suffered from depression, even though they have talked about Elisabeth's episodes.

Her mother admitted to having similar feelings, but would not label them as depression. They have talked about a family member with post-natal depression, and even a character in a book showing signs of depression, but Elisabeth says her mother does not use the label, or recognize the behaviour as depressive.

Elisabeth is very vigilant about not developing addictive behaviours as she is aware of modeling behaviour for her children. This is especially important to her because her children's father (from whom she has been separated for 10 years) is also an alcoholic.

I need to be able to demonstrate to them that it is possible to enjoy alcohol on an occasional basis, without needing to have it every day. However, I have a feeling that it would be VERY easy for me to tip over into drinking every day. (In the past 10 years I have only had enough alcohol to make me drunk three times, and often go for weeks or months without having any alcohol. I can buy a bottle of wine and it will take me three or four days to finish it all.) For depressive behaviour, I try to be aware of when it might start to be a problem again, and try to look after myself at that time. I acknowledge that depression is an illness, and tell my children that I am unwell. I look for signs of depression in them, and try to maintain the channels of communication.

Elisabeth says her children, ages 10 to 19 have not shown signs of addictive behaviour, but she is concerned at times about her sons. One is very withdrawn at times, while the other is very active and has trouble controlling his emotions sometimes. By talking to her children about her feelings, and theirs, Elisabeth hopes that she is keeping the lines of communication open in her family, and with their schools. She has recently had to give up paid work, to spend more time with her 12 year-old son, which is causing financial difficulties, but she is coping.

Elisabeth has recognized a link between depression and alcohol in describing her mother's illness. While she is aware of her risks of becoming alcoholic, she is working very hard not to make that risk a reality.

She recognizes both the hereditary and the environmental factors in dealing with these illnesses. She notes that things are easier now that depression is being recognized more widely as a bona-fide illness in her country.

For their book, <u>Risk and Resilience: Adults Who Were the Children of Problem Drinkers</u>, authors Richard Velleman and Jim Orford interviewed more than 160 participants, and examined a great deal of literature. They stated that previous research was "motivated by the search for specific transmission of drinking problems from one generation to the next". These would include genetic-biological mechanisms, which are being given much more importance now than they were 25 years ago when this type of research was first being done.

Velleman and Orford also state that genetics were thought to play much less a role in determining whether a child of an alcoholic would become an alcoholic than the role played by sociological, peer group, family and other environmental factors.

A number of twin, adoption and other studies have been conducted to establish whether and to what extent alcohol problems may be hereditary.[iii]

Admittedly, genetics do play a role in determining familial patterns with depression and alcoholism. Whether they play more of a role than environment is still being debated among researchers, or so it would seem. It's the old nature vs. nurture argument.

In recent years, some scientists have come to believe that there is, in fact, an "alcohol gene". But they cannot say how dominant it is. Velleman and Orford think it might not be very dominant at all. I tend to agree with them.

While some of my mother's siblings exhibited behaviour that might have been linked to their drinking, others did not. My sister and I share the same genetic codes, yet you could not meet two more different women. We don't even look alike! Our personalities are very different, and she does not fit the "pattern" of having either depression or alcoholism at all! Or, if she does, she is even better at denying it than our mother was!

What is it about my sister that has made her more resilient, or perhaps resistant to depression? She probably just didn't have time for it! She was married at the age of 19, and had three children before her 25th birthday. I got married at the age of 22, but did not have my first child until I was almost 28. Did that just give me too much time on my hands? I think it goes deeper than that, and so do Velleman and Orford. They state that if a child of an alcoholic, has a harmonious life, the child is less likely to fall prey to becoming an alcoholic, or marry an alcoholic (which, according to many studies happens with daughters of alcoholics, especially daughters of alcoholic fathers). This includes a strong network of supportive friends and family.

My sister had that support system when she had her children. I did not. My husband was, for many years, my only real source of constant support. By the time I *had* made a number of friends, and was feeling part of the community, we had another child, and subsequently moved to another town because of my husband's job. I am not laying blame here. It was what it was, and I coped the best I could. In hindsight, I didn't really do it all that well. But, as many women do, I took care of my family first, and me last. My sister also says that my depression developed because I "take things to heart much more deeply" than she does. It's one of our personality differences. I think my sister feels things just as deeply, but she does not have the "chemical imbalances" in her brain that I do, which have been suggested as the cause for my mood disorders.

Lest you think this is all a story of gloom and doom, far from it. I did recognize that I had a lot of dreary days, and did my damnedest to overcome them. I was never "down" for more than a few days at a time, and it might not have been the full part of any given day. When you are a mom to two young boys, the tendency is to put their needs before your own. That keeps you thinking about other things. Perhaps I knew, even then, that I was headed down a path of depression, and was fighting to keep myself away from it.

So, to ask the question posed in my chapter heading again, "are we doomed to repeat the past?" Velleman and Orford don't think so. In fact, they state the following:

The fact that most offspring are not in fact at risk, as far as we can tell, must be communicated along with a balanced statement of the risks offspring do run and an assessment of the other factors such as childhood psychological problems and family disharmony that may moderate the risk relationship.[iv]

While my mother drank when I was a child and teenager, I did not grow up with an alcoholic mother. Her drinking increased, as I said earlier, the more she was alone. As I noticed my mother's alcoholism progressing, there was an increasing fear that I could develop a similar problem. The knowledge of that risk has done just as Velleman and Orford predict: it has strengthened me, and my resolve not to be like her.

I am more aware of all of the physical and psychological side effects of alcohol. It has also made me appreciate the power of the addiction once it takes hold. I think it has done the same thing with my sister. She also drinks alcohol occasionally, but is very aware under what circumstances she is drinking, and how it affects her. We are both very aware of how easily we could"go over to the dark side".

Many offspring, according to Velleman and Orford, are "over-predicted" and their alcoholism becomes almost a self-fulfilling prophecy. Some of their participants also reported being treated "differently" by health and social service providers because they knew of a family member with a drinking problem. That over-prediction, they say, can lead some researchers to conclude that children of problem drinkers should not be told of potential risks. I disagree with that conclusion, as do Velleman and Orford. Just as I need to know the extent of my mother's family problems with heart disease, and my father's familial history with diabetes, so too, I need to be aware of the risks of developing alcoholism and depression. To not be aware of them does a disservice to me, and to my children.

While we may not be doomed to repeat the past, we invariably do, at least to some extent.

Margaret's story:
Margaret says that her mother never talked about being depressed.
but there was yelling, sadness, fury, bitterness, inability to clean or cook at times, or really 'mother us--me and my sister'. She didn't leave the house, had no close friends, and did NOTHING at all, day after day.

That, Margaret thinks, was depression, which her mother later coped with by drinking heavily. She thinks her mother felt isolated in her new role as a mother, first to two stepsons, and then two daughters; leaving her paid work; and living in a rural area. As a reason for her fury, sadness, and bitterness, her mother mentioned all of these at one time or another.

You know, it was me who discovered that all the hidden, empty beer cans and vodka bottles belonged to my mother. I was 15. She had told me they were Dad's. But then I found them, lots of them, tucked in her sewing area. I charged out of the house, and ran around it and around it and around it like a mad woman. Then I threw them all out - bags full. And later confronted my Dad, who never stopped watching the TV when I told him. It was I who, years before, had sat with my mother, with her purple lips (Manneshewitz wine), as she lay passed out on our couch. Her breathing was so shallow, and she looked so odd. I had NO IDEA why she looked that way, only I was sure that if I stopped watching her, she would die. So, day after day, year after year, I watched. And "I" became the one who drank, too. While my sister did not - she is eight years younger than me. She has never drank. Man, I can still see those purple lips and hear that labored breathing. I am 42 and it still makes me weep in fear and sadness.

Margaret worries that her children may develop alcohol problems of their own. Although, at the present time, she says she is "up to her ears in diapers and fingerpaint", so she doesn't really have too much time to think about the future. She hopes that if there are problems, they will be talked about more among her family members than it was between her mother, father, herself and her sister. It was NEVER talked about, she says, and she thinks that if she, or her sister were to raise the issue now, with either parent, it would be denied that there were any problems (there are those three "D's" again!).

Margaret says that she did drink heavily ("like a fish") from her mid-teens to her mid-thirties, and also smoked heavily. When under extreme stress, she would retreat to the world of "junk novels that she says she "wouldn't be caught DEAD reading now". (I wonder if sometimes, she does retreat to that world, just as I retreat to my watching too much television.) She has stopped drinking and smoking, and she does take medication to help with panic and anxiety. Margaret has also taken care of herself by having her depression diagnosed by a physician, and being treated with anti-depressants and therapy. She still has depressive periods if she is under severe stress. With three young children, and her own academic career, Margaret hasn't quite figured out how to "fit in taking care of me", but she does exercise and meditate. She hopes for some tools to figure out how not to become her mother, but not go to the other extreme of being a super-woman either. She says that her mother has done NOTHING in the 40 years Margaret has known her.

I don't know how to explain what I mean by that, but I know that it is VERY important for my sister and I to be super-busy, always moving, always having things that HAVE to get done, especially for others. Otherwise we are terrified we might become our mother. This leaves little time for us to take care of ourselves.

Perhaps, as Velleman and Orford state, Margaret, and her sister are becoming stronger and less demoralized by their past. They will become more hopeful about their future being free of alcohol and depression. It may be something they are not yet aware of fully. From my non- medical and non-scientific observation, I would say that being aware of the risks has definitely made them stronger women, and therefore better able to handle any hurdles in the future. They will find that "happy medium" they seek, and are not doomed to follow on their mother's path, or spin out of control by living at the fast pace they seem to have now.

Margaret talked not only of her mother's alcoholism and her fears of repeating that pattern, but also of her fear of repeating her mother's depressive nature. Like alcoholism, the disease of depression also runs in families.

We are hearing more about depression in the popular press now. A recent issue of the *Rosie* magazine, named for American talk-show host and comedienne Rosie O'Donnell, features several articles about depression, specifically depression in families. O'Donnell herself has suffered from depression. She is only now talking publicly about it, as are other celebrities who share their stories.

In discussing the "nature vs. nurture" argument in the magazine, psychologist Martha Manning notes,

There's no simple cause of depression. Research shows that the illness clusters in families, but it's not the result of genes alone. As with many illnesses, heredity and environment both play a role. Our life experiences leave a mark on our biology; they can strengthen our mental health or leave us more vulnerable to depression. Being sexually abused in childhood for example appears to alter the way our bodies react to stress--a change that persists through adulthood. It's no surprise, then, that the physical and sexual abuse are linked to depression later in life.[v]

In the same issue of the magazine, Manning's daughter Keara Depenbrock talks about mental and physical illnesses she has inherited from her mother.
She says that "one of the reasons I might not get as ill as my she [my mother] did is because of the hard-won knowledge she gained through her own depression." [vi]

Keara's experience shows that there is hope for Elisabeth, Margaret, me, and others like us. I don't think we are doomed to repeat our mothers' past.

When I read Margaret's story, I was saddened, but I also found hope in her voice. I also found humour in her description of being "up to her ears in diapers and fingerpaint". That conjures up quite the picture doesn't it?

Rather than moving at too hectic a pace, to avoid her mother's lethargy, Margaret is learning the slower paces of yoga and meditation, and she is involved with her children's lives--something it seems her mother wasn't able to do.

Elisabeth says her mother doesn't touch alcohol now, and having seen her mother's struggles with alcohol makes Elisabeth and her sister more aware of their risks of having similar problems.

Sometimes, we are still struggling with our past, but hope that with help, we will be able to put some of the demons from our past to rest.

Mora's story:

Basically, I am one of seven children. We have one of those families where nothing is ever talked about. I am the sixth child and was born quite a bit later than the others. They have told me how my mother locked herself in her room for three days when she found out that she was pregnant with me. (I was an accident). Throughout my life, she has had about two glasses of wine every evening, and occasionally would drink beyond that. This is when the fighting with my father ensues. Ironically, she has always criticized those families who drank a lot. I am not sure if I would call her an alcoholic, although my sisters and I have thought that on many occasions. We all know, or think, that my mother is depressed, but she would never admit it--well not to the extent that we think she should, and is not the type to seek help. I think all of my siblings and I have suffered from various forms of depression.

My mother raised seven children without much help, and I have a feeling her upbringing was pretty rough too. I do not think that our family is as tragic as other stories I have heard about depression and alcoholism, but still interesting, especially because we have never framed our family in such terms.

I know this issue is important to me because I have spent this year in therapy, trying to learn that I am not my mother. I guess that I am more at fault for calling her crazy--part of which is her depression. Ouch, that makes me feel bad just writing that.

Knowing that these illnesses might be passed down from our mothers may help to recognize them, explain them, and help with therapy as we discuss them, but it does not mean they cannot be dealt with. Nor does it mean that we can't laugh at them sometimes, like Margaret is doing. I wonder if she's tried fingerpainting on the diapers? After all, laughter, they say, is the best medicine.

Endnotes:

[i] Papolos, Demitri, F., M.D., Papolos, Janice, <u>Overcoming Depression</u>, Third Edition, Harper Collins, 1997, p. 56

[ii] Several women shared their stories of depression and alcoholism. They have shared how these illnesses affected their mother (or in some cases, father), and how they themselves have been affected. These stories appear throughout the book. To protect the women's privacy, I have used only first names, and in some cases, pseudonyms.

[iii] Orford, Jim, and Velleman, Richard, <u>Risk and Resiliance: Adults Who Were the Children of Problem Drinkers</u> (Harwood Academic Publishers, 1999), p. 57

[iv] <u>Ibid</u>, pp. 265-266

[v] Manning, Martha, "Nature vs. Nurture," <u>Rosie</u>, USA Publishing, New York, New York, September 2001

[vi] <u>Ibid</u>, Depenbrock, Keara, "Breaking Free"

CHAPTER THREE

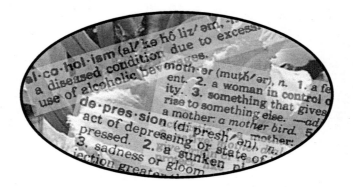

Some Definitions That
May Help

CHAPTER THREE

Some Definitions That May Help

When someone doesn't understand that he is in the throes of a depression, he is likely to ascribe the symptoms to erroneous causes, thereby delaying medical treatment. Not only is he confused, he also doesn't have an adequate explanation for those who are witnessing the changes, and the situation is ripe for myth, misunderstanding and distortion.[i]

As my story, and the stories of some other women show, some forms of depressions may go totally unrecognized, and they can be difficult to diagnose. It might be useful to have some definitions. In this chapter, I have included some reference charts, and other information used by doctors to diagnose depression. I have also included more information about alcoholism.

If everyone gets depressed sometimes, and they do, how can a *period of depression*, or someone *suffering from depression* be recognized?

Periods of depression are characterized by
- depressed or irritable or anxious mood
- poor appetite and weight loss, or the opposite, increased appetite and weight gain
- sleep disturbance: sleeping too little, or sleeping too much in an irregular pattern
- loss of energy: excessive fatigue or tiredness
- change in activity level, either increased or decreased
- loss of interest or pleasure in usual activities
- decreased sexual drive
- physical aches and pains (including headaches, stomachaches, and lower back pain)
- diminished ability to concentrate
- feelings of worthlessness or excessive guilt that may reach grossly unreasonable or delusional proportions
- other psychotic and delusional thinking
- recurrent thoughts of death or self-harm, wishing to be dead or contemplating or attempting suicide[ii]

These symptoms may be present in isolation, or in combination. They may also be present in varying degrees. That is why help is needed from health professionals for an accurate diagnosis and to develop a good plan for treatment. Sometimes, it may take a little time to get a diagnosis and the help needed. (See the Resource List at the end of the book).

Family members may recognize that you are "not happy", or "not yourself", but they may not recognize that you are depressed, and in need of help. Sometimes this is because the signs are not all that obvious. Other times, it may be due to the fact that to admit there is something wrong with you might mean they are worried that there is something wrong with them, or within their relationship to you. A family member may also worry that if they admit *you* are depressed, they will worry that *they* will become depressed.

In her book, <u>Depression: What Families Should Know,</u> Elaine Fantle Shimberg talks about this fear among families.

For those living with a depressed family member under the same roof, life is more difficult and leaves family members in danger of becoming depressed as well. In fact, experts feel that those living with a depressed person have an *80 percent* chance of becoming depressed themselves. [iii]

Shimberg also discusses the two forms of depression that are most common: reactive and endogenous (now called clinical). Reactive depression is just what it sounds like--in reaction to an event or situation (it is also called situational depression).

A person suffering from this type of depression might exhibit prolonged sadness, a loss of appetite or a "loss of a general zest for living". When this occurs, according to Shimberg, the person has gone from just being depressed to suffering from depression.

The endogenous depression Shimberg talks about is much more frustrating for families, because there is no apparent cause. This depression does not follow a specific event, nor is it triggered by situations. It might be characterized by extreme fatigue that is not associated with any physical activity. The person may also suffer from frequent headaches and other pain that radiates to the neck or lower back. There is usually a biological or chemical basis for this depression, and one that only a qualified medical practitioner can diagnose. This is not the time for "self-help". If you or someone you love has shown any of the symptoms of depression, and there does not appear to be any reason for it, get help immediately.

The following stories from Ariella and Carol*[iv] are examples of how these different forms of depression show up. In Ariella's case, she experienced depression following an ectopic pregnancy (where the fertilized ovum is implanted outside of the uterus.)

Ariella's story:
I cried constantly, could not sleep at all, was afraid to be alone, and became short of breath at times. This has not happened since. Now, I feel sad at times, but not really depressed. When I was feeling depressed, I went to a psychotherapist who told me I was probably pregnant at the time. And so I was. The therapy really helped.

My mother also had periods of depression, which she herself recognized. One event seemed to make it worse--the rejection of her friendship by an ex-sister-in-law. She would be lying in bed all the time, distancing herself. There was a lack of communication, and an inability to parent. She was diagnosed as depressed by a doctor, and received individual therapy, medication, and some shock treatment.[v]

I did everything I possibly could to try and change my situation, and I am very conscious of not allowing my children to experience the fear, loneliness, and insecurity of having a depressed parent.

I have not seen any signs of depression in my children, but we talk openly about what happened. I think there is hope for breaking patterns. These are essential terms and practices. Unfortunately, though my mother is better, there are many incidents, and so many symptoms of continued depressed behaviour, and I lose hope of that ever changing. I have changed however, and I am not affected now by any of those previous symptoms.

While Ariella's depression is related to one event, and was situational, her mother's may not be. There may be a deeper problem, or there may be biological or chemical triggers. It is good to know that she is receiving treatment. Ariella says she doesn't think her mother's condition will ever change, but she doesn't say she has lost hope. It is that hope of a better future that keeps the daughters (and likely the sons) of a depressed or alcoholic parent going. I know that is what kept me going. I must have known in my heart-of- hearts that my mother was not going to take better care of herself by getting treatment for her depression and alcoholism, but I kept hoping she would change her way of life. Even when that hope is fading, we never quite let it go. Caring for a depressed mother takes its toll on the "caregiving child". When I would come home after spending a day or two with my mother, it would take me a couple of days to recover fully. I would start to feel depressed myself.

Shimberg explains this in the following way:

It is more probable that the *vulnerability* to reactive depression and endogenous depression tends to run in families.

That means, you may be more likely to suffer from depression than someone with no disposition to it, but it does *not* mean that you will necessarily suffer from depression just because a parent, uncle, or grandparent did. It is possible, however, to experience depression as a learned response to stress and situational circumstances.".[vi]

Ariella seems to recognize the dangers of becoming depressed herself, or having her children become depressed, and as she says, is doing all that is possible to keep that from happening.

Carol's story is much different from Ariella's, and reflects how the different forms of depression affect people in very different ways. She says her mother probably had, and still has depressive periods, but they have never been acknowledged. Carol has been very pro-active in recognizing and treating her depression, which also led to substance abuse, from which she is recovering.

Carol's Story

My depression just appeared around the age of 16. The same is true for one of my children. Big distractions to my depression were going to college and then heading off to Alaska. I eloped and then I had my kids, so that kept me busy until I was around age 30. During those years, I smoked pot, and abused alcohol. I did not get sober until I was 45. In retrospect, the use and abuse of substances kept me alive. I was often suicidal, although I never acted upon those feelings. I gradually crossed the line into alcoholism and problems with other substances. When one of my children was only in Grade 1, they said he was a "problem". I assumed it [his problem] was from my bad mothering--my drinking, etc, and the legacy that my mother was likely depressed. (It turned out he has a learning disability). I started going to a shrink. I've seen the same woman off and on for about 20 years.

I think we (my siblings and I) are all addicts, but I was the only one who chose substances. The others are, in my opinion, addicted to either religion or intellectualism, or both. My mother is a control freak. I doubt she ever acknowledged real depression, much less its root source. She does use some medication, but she says it is for her blood pressure.

I notice that my child who seems to have problems with depression is often visibly "down". We talk about it, and I encourage therapy with him, as it has helped me. He also takes some medication, and so do I. That helps both of us. When I hear about "hope-based research", I think it might be wishful thinking, but I think that breaking the patterns of depression and addiction can be in your chosen attitude.

Carol is talking about three generations of family members with severe depression, and she is clearly worried about her children's future, and her own. However, by taking medication, and going for therapy, there is hope that she and her son will break the illness patterns in her family. Carol's outlook is positive, and she seems to think that is as important as the medication and the therapy.

Ariella experienced her depression during an ectopic pregnancy. Other women also experience depression during pregnancy if it was not their choice to become pregnant at that time. Many women also experience a "post-partum" depression within a few days of giving birth. Once the hormone levels have leveled off, the "baby blues" go away. Other times, they do not, and the following chart[vii] shows a method that doctors use to diagnose the difference between post- partum blues, a depression, and in more serious cases, psychosis.

Differences between Blues, Depression and Psychosis[viii]

	Blues	Depression	Psychosis
Onset	2-7 days after delivery	Anytime during the first 6 months after delivery	Peak onset 2-21 days after delivery
Prevalence	25-85% of new mothers	10-20% of new mothers	1.7 per 1000 deliveries
Course	Mild Self remitting usually within 2 weeks	Disabling and persistent Recovery in 60-70 % of cases within 1st year	Psychiatric emergency hospitalization usually required Good response to appropriate antipsychotic regimen
Symptom Profile	Tearfulness, fatigue, anxiety, sadness, hypersensitivity, poor concentration poor sleep, poor appetite, feeling overwhelmed	Depressed mood, loss of interest, and four of the following-- change in weight, change in sleep, psychomotor agitation or retardation, feelings of worthlessness, poor concentration, recurrent thoughts of suicide	Mania with psychotic symptoms; Psychotic depression or schizophrenia-like psychosis
Treatment	Usually untreated Support and reassurance	As for Major Depressive Episode: Psychotherapy in mild case, decision to use drug therapy should be influenced by severity of episode, breast feeding and prior depressive episodes.	Electroconclusive therapy (ECT) or antidepressant + antipsychotic for psychotic depression; antisychotic agent for psychosis; Mood stabilizer + antisychotic for mania

As the chart shows, there is a variance in symptoms, and not all of the symptoms have to be present for a diagnosis, just the majority of them for a specific diagnosis to be made.

With depression other than post-partum, current research has shown that a number of things, including the influence of gender; age; and sociocultural factors, should be considered.

I found the following information useful when looking at the patterns of depression in my life, and to become aware of risk patterns for my sons. (Fortunately, they have not exhibited any of these symptoms.)

As with the previous chart on depression, some of these symptoms (shown below) may be present, alone, or in combination with others. Only a qualified health professional can determine if depression is present.

It isn't easy being a kid or a teenager. Some angst is to be expected, and is normal. Yes, it's normal for your teenager to constantly have the door closed to his room when he's home and answer you in short sentences. It doesn't mean that he wants to be left alone all of the time though, and some gentle persuasion might be necessary to get him talking if there is a problem. It is worth the effort. I am constantly surprised that my husband and I are sometimes considered to be very good company for my 21 year-old, and he will actually join us for activities. Our 17-year-old will join us too, but not as often. Times spent with our sons are great for conversations about what's going on in their lives.

This information should be considered as a reference only, and not taken as medical information from me. Remember, I told you, I'm not a doctor, (and I don't even play one on TV.) My thanks to my mother's physician for providing this information, and the preceding chart.

Influence of gender:

* prevalence of major depression is greater in boys than in girls before puberty

* women are affected twice as often as men, with the exception of bipolar disorders (characterized by two extremes of moods; also known as manic-depression)

* women tend to seek help earlier in the course of illness and are more ready to report symptoms

* the influence of the menstrual cycle on antidepressant drugs and therapeutic response to those drugs has been understudied

* compliance [with treatment] may be influenced by gender

* males with **sudden** alteration in alcohol consumption may have an underlying depressive disorder

* males and females have comparable course [of treatments] once a diagnosis is made

Influence of Age:

* major depression (or Major Depressive Disorder, using its medical term) is **NOT** a "normal" feature of adolescent behaviour

* early onset Major Depressive Disorder is often preceded by anxiety disorder, or other serious symptoms of depression

* early onset of Major Depressive Disorder is characterized by mood disorders in 1st degree relatives (parents,
siblings)

* common childhood disorders (e.g. Attention-
Deficit/Hyperactivity Disorder (ADHD), and Learning
Disorders can be associated with underlying Depression

Sociocultural Factors:

* prevalences are remarkably consistent across cultures

* perception of depression as an illness differs across
cultures

* many ethnocultural groups may not volunteer symptoms
(these include Asian and Native)

* symptom profiles and intensity of affective expression
vary across cultures

* recent immigrants are at particular risk

When looking at the Symptom Profile, there are additional age related symptoms to be considered:

* irritability is often the predominant external mood
symptom

* "bad" behaviour

* apathy and social withdrawal

* acute decline in school performance

* alcohol and substance abuse

* somatic (sleeping) complaints--either too much or too
little sleep-- and anxiety symptoms

Carol has noticed some of these symptoms in one of her children, and is encouraging therapy and medical treatment. Ariella is sensitive to her children's moods, and they have openly discussed what is happening. This awareness may mean that the children will not develop the same symptoms of depression, or if they do, they will not be as severe.

The women whose stories appear in this book have experienced depression in varying degrees, and for a variety of reasons. Finally, depression is being taken seriously as an illness and not as a character flaw, or a lack of willpower.

Having a family member think you are weak or lazy when you are sick, is very difficult and quite frankly, is maddening. It's enough to drive you crazy! I've heard what writer Susanna Kaysen calls the "Failure of Will" theory from friends and relatives when I've been depressed. Kaysen is the author of Girl, Interrupted, a memoir of her experiences in a psychiatric hospital--it was made into a movie starring Winona Ryder and Angelina Jolie.

The Failure of Will theory is equally popular with people who are not depressed. Get out and take your mind off yourself, they say. You're too self-absorbed. This is just about the stupidest thing you can say to a depressed person, and it is said everyday to depressed people all over this country. And if it isn't that, it's Shut Up and take your Prozac.
These attitudes are contradictory. Conquer Your Depression and Everything Can Be Fixed by the Miracle of Science presuppose opposite explanations for the problem. One blames character, the other neurotransmitters. They are often thrown at the sufferer in sequence: Get out and do something and if that doesn't work, take pills. Sometimes they're used simultaneously: You won't take those pills because you don't WANT to do anything about your depression, i.e. Failure of Will.[ix]

Kaysen goes on to say that sadness should not be eliminated all the time. Depression and despair, she says, "are reasonable reactions to the nature of life." Shit happens, (As the popular phrase goes.)

"We are supposed to feel like hell once in a while," she says. When it goes on and on, or keeps coming back, then something is wrong. We often "know" something is wrong long before a doctor may diagnose it. Consider the following:

In sooth, I know not why I am so sad
It wearies me; you say it wearies you.
But how I caught it, found it, or came by it,
What stuff 'tis made of , whereof it is born,
I am to learn[x]

This passage is from Shakespeare's play, "The Merchant of Venice", written in 1600. It was used almost 400 years later in the opening pages of <u>How to Cope With Depression: A Complete Guide for You and Your Family</u>, written by Keith Ablow, and J. Raymond DePaulo Jr.[xi]

Ablow and DePaulo agree with other medical information about the causes of depression being from one of four areas:

    *pharmacological (from medicines)
    *neuronal (a malfunction of the brain)
    *endocrinological (a glandular problem)
    *genetic (family history)

They state that the genetic causes may be the most significant. Ablow and DePaulo also address the double problem of depression and addiction.

Without withdrawal, they note, it is difficult to accurately diagnose a mood disorder. Complicating this matter is the fact there is sometimes dissention in the medical community as to the best course of treatment for depression.

Around and around it goes. Where it stops, nobody knows. Once again, we have that "vicious cycle" of depression and alcoholism. Alcohol is used to cope with stress, low moods, anxiety, panic, and other symptoms of depression. The alcohol is a depressant, the depressive mood becomes more intense, and more alcohol is used to deal with the intensity. According to Ablow and DePaulo, "people will go to great lengths to escape their emotional pain, and attempts to find peace consumes tremendous energy."

Carol says "she gradually crossed the line into alcoholism". She herself may not have recognized that she had a problem, even though others may have seen it. Or, she may have missed the opportunities to recognize it earlier than she did. Alcoholism can be even more difficult to recognize than depression is, because there are so many variables as to what is "acceptable" behaviour in our society when it comes to the use of alcohol. Also, it is especially difficult once that first "D" has kicked in. I recognize now that I denied my mother's alcoholism for many years. She was *my mother*, and I could not bring myself to admit how sick she was.

Something else to keep in mind is that alcohol reacts differently in women than in men, which is why a woman might say, "well, I only have two or three drinks a night, the same as my husband, and he doesn't get drunk, so I don't either."

"The same amount of alcohol affects a woman more than a man. Alcohol does more physical damage to women more quickly than it does to men.[xii]

This physical damage may have effects on the function of the liver, heart, stomach and brain, according to research done at the Centre for Addiction and Mental Health (CAMH) in Toronto, Canada. There can also be problems with memory, learning and co-ordination. Hormones also cause the water levels in women's bodies to change. (We didn't need the CAMH to tell us that. Just ask any woman who has to keep several sizes of clothes in her closet to accommodate "that time of the month"). But, not only does our body tissue retain more water just before our period, it also retains more alcohol, so we may become drunk more quickly.

Birth control pills affect the way alcohol travels in your system, and when the hormone levels drop after menopause, this causes us to get drunk faster, according to the research.

So, if you are feeling depressed, and think that having a drink might make you feel better, that's likely the last thing you should do. (See the chapter, "Eat, Drink, and Be Merry")

Drinking for women may also be a problem for them because a woman's drinking may be looked upon differently than a man's drinking. Alcoholics are shunned in our society, so both sexes have problems. I am concentrating on our *mothers'* depression and alcohol, so I looked more at the research connected with women's drinking. The CAMH has excellent literature on drinking patterns in men, which may state some of the following information to be just as applicable to men.

Society judges women's drinking problems more harshly than men's. As women, we are expected to live up to the role of child bearer, lover, mother, and caretaker. When we use alcohol to help us cope with these roles, we may be seen as failures.[xiii]

It can be difficult for women [and maybe some men] to get the help they need.

It can be difficult to admit to yourself and others that you have a problem. Many people don't understand the reasons why women have drinking problems. People often judge women with drinking problems more harshly than men. Some people don't want to admit that a woman they know has a drinking problem. Sometimes they want to keep her problem hidden. So these women often don't get the support they need. [xiv]

No one is going to suggest giving up alcohol. Well, ok, lots of people *do* suggest it, because they think that alcohol has no redeeming qualities and does more harm than good. That's a personal judgement call, and one that I am not going to make. However, the CAMH does make recommendations about "safe drinking"--generally nine to 12 drinks per week. Also, they recommend that you not drink if you are trying to conceive, pregnant or nursing.

While drinking might be all right for you, it is definitely NOT okay for babies. (To show how far that thinking has come, my mother told me that grandparents and even doctors used to recommend a shot of whisky to help calm a colicky or fussy baby. In the past 21 years, since I had kids, few, if any, people would suggest such a remedy.) Alcohol *was* a large part of growing up for many of us.

Lee's story:

I cannot recall when my life was not being affected by alcohol. Both my parents were drinkers, and in my mother's case, the drinking continues, although it is probably lighter now than at other times. My father died two years ago in (large?) part due to alcohol consumption. I remember these things in particular about my youth and their drinking:

> *—my father sharing his beer with my brother and me in sparkly plastic cups*
> *—going with dad regularly to pick up and drop off cases of beer; the nice men there would give us lollipops*
> *—being embarrassed in elementary school taking my lunch in what were clearly brown paper bags from the liquor store (the other kids may not have known this, but I did)*
> *—our parents were once so drunk, or hung over, that our Christmas presents came in those brown bags*
> *—the drinking that went along with the Great Books Club meetings*
> *—the increased drinking in the family went on all the time: family dinners; friends or relatives coming over; etc.*

Lee says she and her brother started drinking, and taking recreational drugs when they were in their teens. It seemed natural to them, because of the drinking at home. She remembers thinking how hypocritical it was of their parents, especially her mother, to criticize her and her brother for smoking pot when her parents were drinking on a daily basis. Lee's mother told her that dealing with Lee and her brother in their teenage years was difficult, and she didn't know how to deal with it, so she drank.

Alcohol in the home was perhaps not front and centre, but it had a definite presence, Lee says. There was no fighting, abuse, or lost jobs: scenarios Lee associates with alcoholic homes. She adds that it still makes her angry that she was told her parents did not have the money to buy what *she* needed, but had enough for the alcohol. But a higher price was paid:

I became a heavy drinker (party girl) as a teenager and into my early 20s. I used alcohol to make me feel more confident, to fit in, to overcome shyness, because I felt better when I didn't think too much. I was always what some would call "high strung", and my drinking helped me feel more relaxed. My mother is also an anxious person, and women of her generation often relied on alcohol to smooth things out. I think she was completely oblivious to the role alcohol played in her life, or that her usage of it might be a problem.

I often felt as a child, and still feel as an adult, that I was the more mature of the two of us. I often felt I had to fend for myself and that she was not there emotionally for us kids.....

I still have troubles with self-confidence, self-esteem, relaxation, and so forth. I suffered from anxiety attacks on and off for a number of years, which while not crippling were painful and embarrassing. I never sought help for them because I was so embarrassed, and continued to self-medicate with alcohol and drugs.

Lee says she "finally got her act together" and created a pretty nice life for herself. Her daughter was diagnosed with developmental difficulties, and her husband moved out--bringing on many of the problems Lee had experienced in the past. She was diagnosed with anxiety and depression, and has received therapy, and taken some medication to help improve her health. Her own research into her health problems has led to a number of interesting conclusions, she says, including the role that biology, inherited traits, environment and life circumstances play in the development of anxiety and depression. Lee says "I am slowly finding myself, and my way."

She and her two brothers drink occasionally, but carefully. She thinks the potential for abuse is always there and she does not want to be the kind of parent her parents were.

I want to be there for my daughter, so she can learn to be there for herself--to feel strong and capable and in charge of her life. So far, I think I'm doing a pretty good job.

Living with an alcoholic mother can instill the Fear of God, or at least the Fear of the God of Addiction (if there is such a creature). You are likely to think that *any* drinking is not a good idea out of fear that it will lead you to becoming an alcoholic. As Lee, and many of us, have figured out, while there may be an *increased risk* of a child of an alcoholic having a problem with alcohol, or some other substance, it is not a given. There are a number of other factors to consider. These include gender development and birth order, according to Robert J. Ackerman, author of <u>Perfect Daughters: Adult Children of Alcoholics</u>

There may be a number of other behaviours an "adult daughter" may exhibit, like anxiety, self-esteem problems, and the like, which do not have anything to do with being the daughter of an alcoholic mother. I think what he might be saying here is that just because you walk like a duck doesn't mean you are a duck. You could be a goose!

Your "typology", Ackerman says, is based on where you have been and *contributes* to who you are today, but does not necessarily determine your outcome.

(he never defines "typology", but it is defined as "human behaviour or characteristics according to type" in the Canadian Oxford Dictionary.)

"Therefore, your typology should have nothing to do with predicting your future. Without change, however, it will predict it perfectly."[x]

Although a lot of research has been done in these areas, there is evidence that a lot more is needed, and in fact, *is* being done.

It was commonly thought that patients with mood disorders who use substances were self-medicating - they were either prolonging the highs of hypomania with stimulants or calming anxiety of depression and the irritability of mixed states with alcohol. In the last few years, however, researchers have begun to look more carefully at this 'comorbidity' of substance abuse with mood disorders and are asking the following questions: -Is this association really due to attempts at self-medication? -Is the tendency to crave substances of abuse a heritable phenomenon that travels in the company of the gene or genes that predispose to mania or depression? Or do abused substances induce mania or depression? Whatever the answer, the comorbidity of substance abuse and affective [depressive] illness has been vastly underestimated.[xvi]

I haven't given you much humour in this chapter, but there is hope, I think, that these diseases, and their effects on families, are better understood. While they will continue to be a part of society, we may be able to end them in our own families.

Endnotes:

[i] Papolos, Demitri, F., M.D. and Janice Papolos, <u>Overcoming Depression,</u> Third Edition, Harper Collins, 1997, p. 9

[ii] <u>Ibid</u>, p. 8

[iii] Shimberg, Elaine Fantle,<u> Depression, What Families Should Know</u> (Ballantine 1991), p. 55

*see Endnotes from earlier about the names used for these women's stories

[iv] These are more stories shared with me. Only first names are used to protect the women's privacy

[v] Antidepressant or antipyschotic medication, in combination with therapy and electroconvulsive therapy (ECT--also known as shock treatment) are sometimes used in cases of pyschosis. Only the doctor and the patient can determine the level of success as it is very individual.

[vi]Shimberg, Elaine Fantle, <u>Depression, What Families Should Know</u> (Ballantine 1991

[vii] Clinical Diagnosis of Major Depressive Disorders

[viii] <u>Ibid</u>

[ix] Kaysen, Susanna, "One Cheer for Melancholy", <u>Unholy Ghost: writers on depression,</u> Casey, Nell, Ed., William Morrow, 2001

[x] Shakespeare, William, from the play, "The Merchant of Venice", written in 1600 A.D.

[xi] Ablow, Keith Russell, M.D. and J. Raymond DePaulo Jr., M.D., <u>How to Cope with Depression: A Complete Guide for You and Your Family</u> (McGraw-Hill, 1989), p. 1

[xii] Action on Women's Addictions Research and Education (A.W.A.R.E.) booklet, "Women and Alcohol"
Published by AWARE and the Centre for Addictions and Mental Health (1999) p. 1

[xiii] Action on Women's Addictions Research and Education (A.W.A.R.E.) booklet, "Women and Drinking"
Published by AWARE and the Centre for Addictions and Mental Health (1996) p. 6

[xiv] <u>Ibid</u>. p. 10

[xv] Ackerman, Robert J., <u>Perfect Daughters: Adult Children of Alcoholics,</u> (Health Communications Inc. 1989), p. 95

[xvi] see i

CHAPTER FOUR

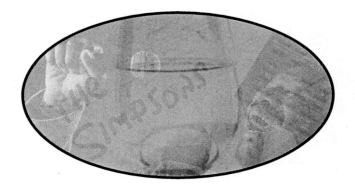

Under The Influence

CHAPTER FOUR

Under The Influence

Okay, so now that we know some definitions about depression and alcoholism, let's look at how they show up not only in our society, but also in the popular culture.

Sex, drugs, and rock 'n' roll. That well-worn phrase is often used when discussing how frequently these are part of the popular culture of rock music. Alcohol and drugs play a significant role in the lives of many artists and the work they produce. They are very evident in many forms of popular culture. In this chapter, I look at the prevalence of those substances in popular culture, and ask, "Are we all under the influence?"

Let's start with music. What is it about rock, the blues, or other music culture that attracts artists to drugs? I posed that question to radio programmer, Ron Dickenson, who offered the following:

Good question! I don't really know. Many musicians have said that they are "driven" by the music "inside" of them and that when it gets too intense, they use drugs (e.g., Charlie Parker). Others get into drugs as a means of dealing with success/pressure (e.g., early Aerosmith); others do it because of peer pressure or they see it as a necessary part of the lifestyle. And of course, why does anyone abuse drugs...? Because they're addictive![i]

Dickenson says that, in his "non-expert" opinion, many artists may have started out using the drugs for "inspiration", and then wound up needing them, almost every day both physiologically and psychologically. He adds that for most of his listeners, who are adults, he is not concerned about any negative influences the music might have on their lives.

Fans, he says, recognize that many of the songs are about the life experiences of the artists. The fans may empathize with the experience, but at the same time, are glad that their experiences may not have been as painful.

When he plays a song that refers to drugs and/or alcohol, particularly their abuse, Dickenson will perhaps comment on the song if there is a special significance between the reference and the music or the artist's life. What does Dickenson think about music's influence in our lives?

I think music is an essential means of communication among all people. Without it, we're not complete and our lives are missing "something".

Music is an essential form of communication, (as are filmmaking and writing). These forms of pop culture: music, movies, and books contain many references to drugs and alcohol use by characters. There are also numerous references on television.

Do these actions by characters, most of whom are fictional, have an effect on our everyday lives? That has been, and likely will continue to be the subject of debate by many. It certainly has been the topic of many dinner-table conversations in my family.

Having alcohol in the house was the norm in my family as I was growing up, and there is usually some alcohol in my house now. In the 50s and 60s the "drink before dinner" was an accepted norm, as was the wine decanter on the dinner table, wine with dinner, and sometimes drinks afterwards. There seemed to be a lot more "social drinking" going on then as opposed to now. Maybe that's just my perception. Drinking was often shown in television and movies in a much more glamorous way.

There would be the "liquor cart", or the sideboard filled with crystal decanters and glasses, waiting for the apéritif or nightcap to be poured. Having a drink upon arriving home was the pattern for most characters--even Beaver Cleaver's father drank. [On the late 1950s TV show "Leave It to Beaver"] He'd have his drink, his pipe, and his paper as he waited for Beaver's Mom to get supper ready. My dad didn't have the pipe, but a drink and the paper were definitely part of his before-dinner ritual.(My sister remembers learning to make a "mixed drink" at the young age of 10) Was art imitating life, or was it the other way around?

Another popular movie from that time, "Cat on A Hot Tin Roof", based on the play by Tennessee Williams, featured Brock (Paul Newman) the oldest son in a wealthy family. He had been a football star, and was now injured and could no longer play. He felt like a failure, and drowned his sorrows in alcohol. His wife Maggie (Elizabeth Taylor) scorned by her husband's inability to show his love for her, looked elsewhere for comfort, and was nicknamed "the cat". She also drank to soothe her loneliness.

While that particular story may not have played itself out in many homes, the act of using alcohol to prop up one's ego, or use it to soothe a bruised ego, surely was often done. Seeing it done in a popular play and movie may have given the use of the alcohol in the average family some legitimacy.

The use and abuse of legal substances made for interesting subject matter in movies of the 1950s and early 1960s. These include "The Days of Wine and Roses", and "The Valley of the Dolls". In the first, alcohol was the poison of choice, while pills, and to some extent, alcohol were the culprits in the other movie.

In "Days" Joe (Jack Lemmon) is a "social drinker who loved to socialize". He goes to the bar "with the boys" after work, and ultimately stays too long for his own good, winding up drunk. His wife Ann (Lee Remmick), feeling lonely at home, asks that they socialize together, and before long, she too is hooked on the alcohol. Joe faces the choice of saving his life or saving his marriage. I won't give away any more of the plot, but will say that you will need a few tissues to get through this one.

When I first saw this movie, with my mother, she said could identify with the characters, because, she said, they reminded her of people she knew. The people she referred to perhaps did not go out and get drunk every night, but they frequented bars, and left their families alone. Sometimes, the women also started to drink more, although they would do it more at home than out in the bars, she said.

Perhaps that is why the movie was so successful, both at the box office and with critics. It could be "almost anyone" in the film. Lemmon was playing the "everyman" he so perfected.

Couples struggling with everyday life would see this couple, and think that perhaps their life own life was not really so bad, because they did not need to resort to alcohol to cope. Or at least they didn't use alcohol to the same extent.

In "The Valley of The Dolls", based on the book of the same name by Jacqueline Susann, three women slowly succumb to abusing pills and alcohol to cope with their lives. The book was supposedly based on a side of Hollywood life Susann had known as a struggling actress.

The story follows the careers of three young women. Anne, Neely, and Jennifer--all involved with acting, modeling, and singing. Each of them starts out in their careers with youth and innocence on their side. As the pressures of their careers take their toll, each of them becomes addicted to various types of pills, which they refer to as "dolls".

Neely first takes diet pills, to conform to the "thin is in" life in Hollywood, and pills to either pep her up to keep up with a grueling schedule of voice and acting lessons. She then needs more pills to help her sleep. Before too long, she is hooked. She learns that the pills work faster if you take them

with alcohol, in spite of warnings of ill conse-
quences of this action from her friends. Before
long, Neely has passed on her love of the "dolls" to
Anne and Jennifer.

Was it art imitating life for actress Patty Duke, who
portrayed Neely? During the time of filming this
movie, the actress was constantly taking pills to
either keep her going, or help her calm down. Duke
discusses this in her autobiography, <u>Call Me Anna</u>.[ii]

The movie came to Duke, whose real name *is* Anna
Marie Duke, at a time she was struggling to be
taken seriously as an adult performer after a
successful career as a child and teenager ("The
Miracle Worker", stage play and film, and "The
Patty Duke" show on television).In Duke's opinion,
the book was superior to the film. This superiority,
she said was evident in the book's "pop psychological approach to exploring what it was in the
life-styles of its characters that drew them into their
addiction." She added that playing "someone so
seemingly stable and bright who could get sucked
into such a destructive life-style, was instinctively
appealing to me". The "Neely" character was
reputedly based on Judy Garland, who by that time
in 1965, had her own battles with both alcohol and
drugs. Art was imitating life.

What was not known at the time of filming, was the
fact that she was mentally ill, in need of both medication to regulate her moods, and therapy to deal
with her the effects of her moods, and her past as
an abused child.

Duke was, according to her autobiography, embarrassed by that time in her life, which included a lot of dramatic and traumatic behaviour later attributed to manic-depression, which was diagnosed in 1982.

In <u>Call Me Anna</u>, Duke describes her father's struggle with alcohol, and her mother's periods of depression. She says she has tried, in her life, and in her work, she says, to honour her parents, by bringing public awareness to the diseases of depression and alcoholism.

Addiction to the pills was something Jacqueline Susann apparently also knew about. She had been diagnosed with cancer (from which she died in 1974) and was taking a lot of medication, including her "dolls" to cope with her illness.

"The Days of Wine and Roses" and "The Valley of the Dolls" were two very popular examples of characters being, as Duke put it, sucked into destructive life-styles.

What I find interesting is that what made these movies popular is the fact many people may have identified with these characters. Illegal drugs, e.g. heroin and cocaine, often associated with the "stars" were not readily available or used in those days. Alcohol was readily available, and pills were accessible through doctors. They were perfectly legal, and therefore might have been seen as less harmful than the illegal substances. Now, *those* drugs have taken their place in pop culture, along with another popular drug from the 60s, LSD.
I can't talk about popular culture and not mention "The Simpsons." (Homer Simpson's oft used "d'oh" has even made its way into the lexicon.)

This show has used its popularity well in discussing drugs and alcohol in society. Marge is usually the "moral authority". Homer talks about drinking more than he seems to do it, but he does enjoy his beer. On one show, she asked him to stop drinking for one month. He does, although he sees images of his beer everywhere. After the month's end, he goes to the bar, and sees his cronies in their usual positions at the bar, many of them drunk. He decides he would rather spend time with Marge.

To me, this shows the producers' awareness of the possible influence the show might have on its younger viewers. We likely shouldn't take this too seriously, because it is a cartoon, but it is an important part of popular culture, and people *are* paying attention.

Getting back to reality, many actors, musicians, and literary figures have had their battles with both the legal and illegal substances. Sadly, a lot of them have died, many while they were still at the top of their game. Others may be suffering from latent effects of the drugs used in their younger years. The stories of many of these artists have been immortalized in film. They include "Lady Sings the Blues" (Billie Holiday); "The Charlie Parker Story"; "Me and My Shadows"(Judy Garland, based on the book by her daughter Lorna Luft); "Fire: The Life of Jim Morrison"; and "The Rose", which was inspired by the work of Janis Joplin. Perhaps one of the strangest films, or most unusual, was The Who's "rock opera" "Tommy", where alcohol, drugs, and sex all play a major role in the development of title character Tommy. There is *nothing* subliminal about the drug references in these movies. They show

how much drug use was, and is still a major part of our culture.

References and effects of drugs are certainly evident in many popular songs. My sons have often asked, "what was he on when he wrote that?" when listening to some of the music of my youth: The Beatles, Rolling Stones, Bob Dylan, and others. It is interesting that there was debate then about song lyrics being too explicit about drugs, and the debate continues today.

Are we, as Dickenson says, being hypocrites if we worry about the influence of song lyrics on today's youth when we scoffed at our parents for raising similar concerns with our music? Is there a direct cause-and-effect relationship between song lyrics and behaviour? Are the lyrics of today's artists really any worse than those of the artists of "our day"? (Oh, I sound old don't I? "Back in my day, sonny.....)

Aren't there many other factors to consider? Don't parents, peers, and values learned at home and school have just as much influence on behaviour as do song lyrics, music video scenes, movies, and books? How much influence does our popular culture have on our day to day interactions in our family and community? These heady questions are the subjects of much more intense research than I am doing. My quick answer is: It depends. Nothing is black and white, only shades of gray. Or is it a Whiter Shade of Pale? Baby Boomers will get that reference. The rest of you will have to ask your parents!
Why are so many creative people drawn to "the dark side"? What is it about the creative process

that makes artists, including writers, susceptible to depression and/or substance abuse?

One musician (who prefers to remain anonymous) told me that it had nothing to do with the arts, but the way that an artist's brain is wired. (I can never keep it straight whether artists are right-brained or left-brained. Maybe we're all scatterbrained!) These are his thoughts about drugs, alcohol, and artists:

Quite often, artists feel that they don't belong, even as children. So, they find different outlets to express themselves. They also tend to be rule-breakers and risk-takers. It's not the craft that draws them to the drugs, but the drugs are part of that world that requires rules to be broken and risks to be taken, and some artists are drawn to that aspect.

Most artists I know, including visual artists, musicians, and writers see themselves as oddballs. They are just trying to fit into society. When they feel isolated, they may turn to the drugs to cope with their feelings of being different from everyone else. When they become accepted into a community of other artists, they want to keep that feeling of acceptance, so they might start using drugs, or drinking, if that is what everyone else is doing.

Certain artists may use the drugs to unblock the creative process, but they quickly learn that they can't work when they are stoned or roaring drunk, so they save the substances for the partying, and there is a lot of partying that goes on. But really, all the artist is looking for is what everyone is looking for: acceptance and a way to express themselves. And that may include drugs or alcohol.

The invasion of drugs into our society is also outlined in the recent movie "Traffic" In the telling of three related stories we see how the manufacture, sale and use of drugs, specifically heroin and cocaine affect the lives of a several people. These include a police officer in Mexico, a college student in Ohio, her father, whose job is to "fight the war on drugs" for official Washington, and the wife of a man whose illegal drug business has him in jail. For each of them, the intoxication of money, power, and drugs bring feelings of acceptance to them. Several dilemmas are presented, and like life, there are no easy answers in this art piece.

We can sit and look at such films, and think they are not a part of our lives. We may say, "Well, I don't take drugs, so this doesn't affect me." It may not directly but it may affect the way you think about drug use.

* Is there a difference between the parents who "experimented" with drugs when they were in college in the 60s and their now college-age children?

* Why is it that the parent who has a drink, or two or three, does so in the comfort of their own middle-class home, but their children have to go to a run down part of town to illegally obtain their drugs?

* Is there a difference between the adult who takes a drink to cope with the pressures of work and the student who drinks or smokes a joint to cope with the pressures of school?

* If there is money to be made by trafficking in heroin or cocaine, and that money is needed to maintain a legitimate business and way of life, do you keep the illegal business going?

* If more money is available by helping corrupt politicians and drug traffickers than by working at a job where you *aren't* part of everyone's cor-

ruption, why not join the corruption, especially if it helps your friends?

∗ If you become involved in the corruption, even only temporarily, in order to right past wrongs, does the end justify the means?

All of these questions are posed, by the characters' actions, in the movie "Traffic". While it may not have a direct effect on behaviour, there is no doubt, *some* influence on popular thought in our culture, and in debating the use of drugs in society.

"Traffic" is the kind of movie that is *supposed* to make you think about these things, and it does its job very well. I'm not trying to get a job as a movie reviewer. I'm just trying to show the huge impact that drugs do have on our lives, and how this is reflected in movies.

What movies, such as this, may serve to do is act as a wake-up call to those who watch them. If the subject matter of drugs, or the music of the performer, draws us to see the movie, the portrayal of the addict will, I hope, wake us up to the dangers of drug use. Their seduction of feeling good, feeling powerful, and in some cases, earning lots of money may entice us. The lifestyle of the rock star, actress, or author, might seem appealing, if that glamorous lifestyle includes the abuse of drugs or alcohol, we might just think the price of that lifestyle is one we can't afford.

Perhaps we aren't under any influence or illusions after all. Or are we? My musician-friend says we are all looking for a little peace and serenity.

For thousands of years, many have sought something to alter their perceptions of reality. That includes religious rituals, meditation, and substances. Even if we removed all of the references to these in all of the forms of popular culture, people are still going to look to escape the planet one way or another. Some need to do it on a more regular basis than others do, and they will find a way to do it, regardless of other influences. Sometimes, those escapes can help you to accept who you are and help you come to terms with it. When you return to your reality, whatever that is, you are a happier person. The artist recognizes and expresses that realty, and applies it to their craft. We all have choices to make though.

Looking back on life can be both illuminating and troublesome. It can help put things into perspective, or it can really have a negative impact and prevent moving forward. Looking at my life within the context of popular culture sometimes helps me to find that perspective. It helps if I am able to find something from a book, movie, or song that says, "Yes, someone else understands this." I felt that way when I read the following passage from Patty Duke's book: I wish I could thank her for writing this.

Looking back at the ebb and flow of my life, it exhausts me in precisely the way you get tired when you hear someone else talk about a particularly daunting trip they took. Because so much of it now seems to have happened to someone else. I know that history is part and parcel of my being, but I can't feel the pain anymore, and I can remember wondering if that would ever happen.
And there's another part of me that's really tickled by the whole thing, that can say, "Yup, wasn't that funny? Wasn't that terrible? Isn't it amazing that I survived at all?"
I'm still my own harshest critic and most demanding taskmaster, but I have moved into a time of being much more accepting of whoever it is I am. I have horrible times, I have great

times, I have so-so times, but I wouldn't trade my life today for anyone's, not anyone's.[iii]

While the effects some pop culture may have on society, much of it has a very positive impact, and aren't we all just looking for a good time?

Endnotes:

[i] Dickenson, Ron, Programmer and Host, "Buff Blues", CFRC Radio, Queen's University, Kingston, Ontario, Canada
[ii] Duke, Patty, and Turan, Kenneth, Call Me Anna: The Autobiography of Patty Duke, Bantam Books, 1987, p.178
[iii] Ibid, p. 311

CHAPTER FIVE

Eat, Drink and
Be Merry

CHAPTER FIVE

Eat, Drink and Be Merry

Is it possible to be addicted to chocolate? According to a recent study in the *International Journal of Eating Disorders,* yes! Researchers in Finland found that "chocolate addicts" exhibit the same type of addictive behaviours as other types of addicts--powerful cravings and out-of-control behaviour.[i]

Carrying on with the popular culture theme for a bit, the movie "Chocolat" certainly showed society's love affair with chocolate. Why is it that chocolate is considered so decadent, so sinful? In the movie, the townspeople act very strangely, and out-of-control--behaviour attributed to addiction.

Ann Douglas, author of <u>The Incredible Shrinking Woman--The Girlfriend's Guide to Weight Loss</u> (quoted above), found in doing her research for the book that when men are depressed, they crave high-fat foods like pizza or hot dogs. What do women crave? You guessed it--chocolate.

I don't have to tell you that cravings for fat, sugar, carbohydrates, or salt are very common with women. It's somehow comforting to know that men get them too.

We seem to crave carbohydrates and chocolate the most, especially when we are in the throes of PMS (pre-menstrual syndrome), menstruating, or pregnant. I don't know anyone who has craved strange combinations of food like pickles and ice cream, so often seen in movies and television, but I *do* know that lots of women get food cravings!

I used to get terrible cravings for chocolate and once went to the store at *midnight* to get a chocolate bar! (My brother-in-law was returning a video, and I went with him so I could get the chocolate bar)

I've also sent my kids to the store to get me a chocolate bar to satisfy that craving. My son Jeremy said once (very gleefully as I was giving him the money to get both of us the candy)," Hmm, these chocolate cravings might work in my favour". Since I had a hysterectomy in January 2000, I do not get them as intensely, but curiously enough, I *do* still get the craving for chocolate, about twice a month. I guess my brain is still sending those signals.

According to the research Douglas quotes in her book, foods high in fat and sugar stimulate the production of endorphins, the natural opiate-like compounds in the brain that make us feel better. Exercise supposedly will do the same thing, but it just doesn't seem the same does it?

Cravings for carbohydrates are due to a drop in the levels of seratonin, the hormone that makes us feel good. Carbs supposedly stimulate the brain to produce the seratonin. So, we go for that extra slice of bread, or a larger serving of pasta than we might otherwise eat. At least that's what I tend to do.

Does food affect mood? And, what effect does mood have on what we choose to eat? My husband used to say that he could sometimes tell my moods by what was for dinner. If the meal looked well thought out, and prepared in an interesting way, he knew I was feeling pretty good. If we were having soup and sandwiches, *again*, then he would know things weren't so good. Of course, it gets more complicated than that, but that's a simple example of how being depressed can affect how and what you eat. Not that there's anything wrong with a soup-and-sandwich dinner--in fact it can be a very nutritious and filling dinner.

Eating too much, or not enough, are symptoms of depression. If we are self-medicating the depression with alcohol, as some of us have done, or as our mothers have done, then we get filled up with the alcohol, and don't eat well because we either aren't hungry, or worse, we're too drunk. Alcohol can also make us eat more by increasing the appetite and decreasing willpower (to stay away from food), according to Douglas.

My mother would often go without proper meals, and choose instead to continue to drink and snack while watching television. Unless potato chips are part of a food group, I don't think her snack choices would count as part of a healthy diet. In her last weeks at home, we were convinced that she lived on instant coffee, cigarettes, and of course, her rye- and-water, in spite of the fact there were frozen dinners ready for her to heat. She had lost the will, and the energy to take care of herself properly.

Often when our eating is out of control, whether we are not eating enough, or eating too much, it is because our lives are out of control. Recent research with young women suffering from anorexia showed that the reason they would not eat, even if begged to eat by their friends and family, was that eating, or not eating, was the one area of their lives over which they felt they had some *control* .

Someone who knows a lot about eating when feeling out of control is Sarah Ferguson, the Duchess of York--or the "Duchess of Pork", as she was once dubbed by the British tabloids, because her weight had "ballooned". At the time of the name-calling, "Fergie" was having difficulties in her marriage to Prince Andrew, and difficulties with other members of the Royal Family and their staff. In her book, Dining With the Duchess, (done with staff from Weight Watchers Inc., for whom Sarah Ferguson is a spokesperson), the Duchess writes that during that difficult time she felt alone and humiliated. She felt she had hit rock bottom, and she turned to food for comfort.

Who hasn't had that experience? Eating usually makes us feel better, especially if we are eating our favourite foods. Whether those foods are really good for us usually doesn't matter--we just want to feel better. There are even certain foods: potatoes, bread, gravy, meat loaf, spaghetti, etc. that are called "comfort foods". It probably isn't a coincidence that those foods are high in carbohydrates, reputedly responsible for producing that "feel-good" hormone, seratonin.

In 1992, when I was suffering from depression, and taking the anti-depressants (which did make me feel better, but I think it was a false sense of feeling better, because I never really figured out what was wrong.), I was diagnosed with something called "reactive hypoglycemia". In simple terms, it's low blood sugar, and it is on the diabetes spectrum. My dad was diagnosed in the same month with high blood sugar, which has developed into full-blown diabetes. His mother and sister were also diabetic, with his sister also having the low-blood sugar. My doctor told me that to avoid getting diabetes after the age of 60, I should start a regime of eating six times a day, and watching my weight. "Yeah", I said, "I'll watch my weight get out of control, and I'll be fat!". I've had to learn that eating six times a day does not mean having six full meals a day. What it means is eating more frequently, maintaining a safe level of blood sugar by taking something from each meal and eating it at "snack time". (e.g. have toast mid-morning, instead of with breakfast.

I've since wondered if the anti-depressants that I started taking a few months prior to this diagnosis of low blood sugar were partially responsible for that diagnosis. My blood sugar now is on the low side of normal, as my doctor puts it, but it has not been as low as it was that year. Makes me want to go *hmmmmm?*

Maintaining a healthy weight by exercising and eating a balanced diet is good for us, whether we have this pre-disposition to depression or not. You don't need me to tell you that. Fresh fruits and

vegetables, whole grains, protein, carbohydrates---
yada, yada, yada, as Jerry Seinfeld would say--we
all know what's good for us. *Doing* it is a whole different matter!

We <u>know</u> the drill. So <u>why</u> don't we do it? Because
we just don't *feel* like it! **But**--and this is a big **but**--
this is the one area where, if we are going to
change, if we want to lead healthier lives, we have
to literally get off our **butts**!

Anti-depressant medication can help us get moving.
In her book, <u>The Wisdom of Menopause</u>, Dr.
Christiane Northrup, (who is also the author of
<u>Women's Bodies, Women's Wisdom</u>,) says that
while depression does not affect women of
menopausal age (usually around age 50), as much
as once thought, depression is still a concern for
them. She has some suggestions for treatment for
women of all ages, including taking an anti-depressant for a short time.

Optimally, the medicine will result in a gradual lifting of your
depression. This will give you the energy to mobilize your
own resources to make positive changes in your life.[ii]

Northrup offers the following suggestions for making those positive changes:

> ***Stop drinking.*** Alcohol consumption can make depression
> particularly persistent. This is partly because alcohol is
> itself a depressant, and partly because women too often
> use alcohol as a way to suppress their feelings.

> ***Engage in regular exercise.*** Exercise changes brain
> chemistry (by increasing beta-endorphins, lowering
> catecholamines, and increasing monoamines.), and both
> aerobic and non-aerobic forms have been known to

be helpful in individuals with mild to moderate depression....Exercising twenty to thirty minutes per day, four to five days per week can have a significant positive effect on your mood. It doesn't matter what you do--even dancing around the house to the radio will help.

Get outside in the natural light as much as you can. This helps combat seasonal affective disorder (SAD) and raises your brain levels of seratonin naturally. In the winter, you may need a light box or full-spectrum lightbulbs to get enough light.

Take a good multivitamin that supports your body and brain, and make an effort to eat well. If you are to function optimally, it is important that your brain gets balanced levels of seratonin, essential fatty acids, and glucose. Avoid refined carbohydrates, eat protein at least three times a day, and be sure to include a source of healthy fat in your diet regularly. Eating balanced amounts of complex carbohydrates (with protein) provides the body with appropriate amounts of tryptophan, a building block of seratonin.

Avoid frequent consumption of caffeinated beverages and refined sugar. There is evidence to suggest that they play a role in recurring depression.

Be sure to give your medication a chance to work. Half of those who stop taking their medication within three months of starting get depressed again. To avoid this, it's a good idea to stay on your medication for a minimum of six months, if your depression is severe enough to warrant this approach in the first place.

Northrup later states that the medication should only be used for short periods of time to help us over the bridge to a healthier life, but that we shouldn't live on that bridge. Her research shows I wasn't just making that stuff up about endorphins and seratonin!

While I said there wasn't a *lot* of medical information in this book, there is *some*, which should be discussed with a health professional.

Why don't I just say, "doctor" instead of "health professional"? I believe that there are a number of people who can help us maintain a healthy life. They include medical doctors, chiropractors, registered massage therapists, yoga and reiki trainers, naturopaths, homeopaths, and nutritionists. It can be costly to see some of these practitioners as their particular treatments may not be covered under provincial health plans (although some extended health care plans may cover part of the cost). These treatments are discussed in more detail in the next chapter.

Some of these practices fall under the umbrella of "Alternative Treatment", because it is outside of the type of treatment we know as "conventional", which usually means medical doctors. Many doctors do not have the training or background to understand the benefits of using vitamins and other supplements to help you feel better, so a lot of research is needed. We also have to get away from the notion that there is a pill for everything, and by taking a pill, we will feel better. These other treatments are better than taking pills any day, as far as I am concerned.

One of the most misunderstood food ingredients in our society is soy, although it is starting to get a better reputation. Mention tofu and my family will head for the nearest fast food joint! I have, however, used a soy-based meat alternative successfully in dishes like lasagne and chili. This "veggie ground round" looks enough like hamburger to satisfy the carnivores, and gives me the soy I need for added estrogen and protein, so every-body's happy. I also eat soy meats, such as hamburgers and hot dogs. Soy comes in many forms, and can be used in a variety of interesting dishes--everything from appetizers to desserts. Check out a library or health food store for a good cookbook.

Soy is a regular part of a Japanese diet, and incidences of Alzheimer's disease and dementia are much lower than they are in North America. Soy has also been studied for its effect on your cardiovascular system (heart and lungs) with positive benefits. If eating soy can improve brain and body function, it will help us stay on that road to a long, healthy, happy life. So pass the veggie burgers!

Supplements also have their place in a healthy diet. Northrup recommends supplements to combat depression, and she says that deficiencies of calcium, copper, magnesium, and the omega-6 fatty acids may also relate to depression. She suggests adding the following supplements to the diet:

> Vitamin B-6 and other B-complex vitamins;
> Vitamin C
> DHA (docosahexaenoic acid
> St. John's Wort
> Valerian
> Ginko
> Inositol
> 5-HTP

The dosages, benefits, and side-effects of all of these are well-documented in Northrup's books, and in other literature.

However, as Northrup writes:

Remember, each of the suggestions above works well in some
people but not in others. This is true whether you opt for
medication, exercise, psychotherapy, nutritional supplements,
or another approach. You need to be willing to experiment in
order to find the approch that seems to beckon to you.[iii]

It is possible to become just as addicted to the
so-called "natural" supplements as it is to be
addicted to any other substance. They have their
own side-effects, and have to be taken carefully to
avoid negative interactions with food and drink. You
have to, as Northrup says, be willing to experiment
a little in finding the right combination of foods,
supplements, etc. that affect brain function and
mood.

Brains are like muscles, Northrup says. If we want
it to stay in peak form, we have to use it regularly.
She lists things that help keep the brain functioning
well, and things that the brain doesn't need, such
as aluminum, and aspartame. There are studies to
suggest that by maintaining healthy brain function,
we can preserve mental health and vitality--which
will help keep us from slipping back into the big
black hole known as depression. In addition to
keeping our bodies working well, we have to feed
our brains. (I don't think that's what Grace Slick
from the Jefferson Airplane was referring to when
she sang "Feed Your Head". Another baby boomer
reference I just couldn't resist!)

So here we go again with the low-fat diet, zinc,
vitamins B, C, and E, and all of that good stuff.
Douglas (Ann, the author mentioned earlier) offers
tips for "mastering the art of maintaining your
weight".

You may agree with me that they also apply to maintaining a healthy attitude:

> Don't deprive yourself.
>
> Don't kid yourself.
>
> Stay active.
>
> Pay attention to your body's early warning signals.
>
> Have confidence in your ability to maintain your weight loss (or good mental health).[iv]

Make sure to reward yourself regularly for maintaining your good health. This might include special foods like chocolate cake, or it might include a new piece of clothing, or just time away from your regular work for a while. It doesn't have to cost a lot of money, or take a lot of time, but it does have to be done regularly. As I see it, not doing so is the same as doing work for which you are supposed to receive remuneration, and then not getting paid. There has to be a pay-off for all of the hard work!

Paying attention to your body's early warning signals is important. Knowing the "trigger foods" that may set off another episode of depression (too much coffee, cola, sugar, cheese, chocolate---whatever it is), and knowing the behaviour triggers (watching too much television is mine) is important. Margaret, whose story is part of Chapter Two, read trashy novels when she was under too much stress. We need to watch for those signals, and get help when needed.

We need to trust ourselves, and have confidence in our ability to take care of ourselves. So many of the women who shared their stories with me told me that they are still having trouble fitting "taking care of me" into their schedules. I know, it's easier for me now that our sons are grown. I am inspired by women who take very good care of themselves, and (I think) their lives are busier than mine at times. I figure if they can do it, so can I. I am also inspired by the other women in this book, at the way they have turned their lives around.

One last bit on eating, drinking and being merry. It's important to celebrate the special occasions in your life, and those occasions usually involve food and drink. Go ahead! My sons and my husband always ask for chocolate cake with chocolate icing *and* chocolate ice cream for their birthdays. I try and serve a homemade cake, but sometimes I get the cake from a bakery. That doesn't matter. What matters is that we have this special food to celebrate their birthdays. I usually have a glass or two of wine with the birthday dinner too--going all out!

Yes, I have a predisposition for diabetes, so I shouldn't eat that much sugar. I also have the predisposition for alcoholism, so maybe I shouldn't have the wine. Even with these "no-no's", I will maintain a healthy weight and healthy attitude. I'll be back to my regular life the next day. My food cravings, my moods, and my weight don't control me, I control them. It's important that the special occasions in your life, especially birthdays, are celebrated, and not ignored, even if you celebrate alone. So, as Marie Antoinette said, "Let them eat cake".

The Duchess of York no longer lets food control her either. She says she has helped control her moods, and her weight, by changing her attitudes towards food.

Nowadays, food is not the enemy. I am not fearful of every forkful. Rather, I now use food as a way to control my life....I know that if I can control my weight and food intake, it changes my mood for the day.
It is comforting to know that you can rearrange your thinking, and readjust your habits, that you can change. I am happy to say that I have changed. Rock bottom seems like a long time ago. Nowadays, I rather like the view from up here[v].

So do I.

Endnotes:

[i] Douglas, Ann, <u>The Incredible Shrinking Woman-The Girlfriend's Guide to Weight Loss</u>, Prentice Hall, 2000, p. 47
[ii] Northrup, Christiane, M.D., <u>The Wisdom of Menopause</u>, Bantam 2001, p. 308
[iii] Ibid, p. 313
[iv] Douglas, Ann, <u>The Incredible Shrinking Woman-The Girlfriend's Guide to Weight Loss</u>, Prentice Hall, 2000, p. 138
[v] Ferguson, Sarah, and Weight Watchers International Inc., <u>Dining With The Duchess</u>, Simon and Schuster, 1998, p. 12

CHAPTER SIX

Moving Forward

CHAPTER SIX

Moving Forward

You grieve you learn
You choke you learn
You laugh you learn
You choose you learn
You pray you learn
You ask you learn
You live you learn[i]

Live and Learn. Hindsight is 20/20. One day at a time. Keep it simple. Have a nice day. Take care. All of the clichés fit here don't they? While they may sound trite, they are true. The phrase "take care" is one that while over-used, really does mean something to me now.

I won't say that it is a daily struggle, but it is a struggle. I wish that I didn't have to worry about whether I will become depressed again, or whether

I will become an alcoholic. Perhaps "worry" isn't the right word, because I don't *worry* about it. However, I do think about it. I have to. It is part of my genetic code, and I may not be able to change that, but I can alter how I deal with that history. I choose moving toward a healthy future.

Denying that there is a problem is, or could be, very easy. I could just say, "I am not my mother", and "I will not become my mother". Wishing it, or even saying it, is not enough. Action is needed. The women who share their stories in this book are taking action. They are taking care of themselves, and their children. I am doing the same.

In this chapter, I'll tell you about some of the ways we stay healthy. These include support groups, psychotherapy, herbal remedies, meditation, chiropractic care, and the healing arts of yoga, massage therapy, reiki, and therapeutic touch. These therapies have worked for us, and they might work for others. They might not. Or they might work sometime, but not all of the time. Hey, it's worth a shot--to use another cliché.

Support Groups

Support groups can be lifelines, or they can be sinkers. If sharing our stories with others living with similar illnesses genuinely helps us, it can be a relief. Members of a support group can comfort each other, and they gain knowledge from others' experiences. Quite often, the leader or facilitator in the group, or the members, can provide resource materials such as books or videos to use at home.

By the same token, if all we are hearing is stories of pain and despair, and no stories of hope, it can be very demoralizing, and depressing. Isn't that what we're trying to get away from? I've been to groups where there almost seems to be a *competition* in telling the stories--everyone is trying to make their situation sound worse than the person before them, in order to gain more sympathy from the people in the group.

I found going to Al-Anon meetings difficult because it was keeping the problem of my mother's drinking right in front of me. It was easier to try and forget about her alcoholism between visits, which were not all that frequent as it took more than two hours to drive to her house. I could limit my contact by phone to hours I knew she might be sober. Going to the meetings meant I might have to talk about it, and I wasn't ready to do that. I was still in denial. I did find reading their literature helpful. There are numerous pamphlets and books, as well as other resources. (See Resources)

One of the pamphlets I read from Al-Anon is called "Just For Today". Two of the stanzas had special significance to me.

Just for today, I will be happy. This assumes to be true what Abraham Lincoln said, that "Most folks are as happy as they make up their minds to be."
Just for today, I will have a quiet half-hour all by myself, and relax. During this half-hour, sometime, I will try to get a better perspective of my life.[ii]

One of the most useful things I learned from Al-Anon was that this [the alcoholism] was a family problem. My mother was the alcoholic; there was *nothing* I could do to change that. If she was going to change her habits, the decision to change had to be hers, and she had to want to make it. I had to learn to detach:

Detachment is neither kind nor unkind. It does not imply judgement or condemnation of the person or situation from which we are detaching. It is simply a means that allows us to separate ourselves from the adverse affects that another person's alcoholism can have upon our lives.

Detachment helps families look at their situations realistically and objectively, thereby making intelligent decisions possible[iii]

Adult Children of Alcoholics groups also offer support and information. I have not had any experience with this type of group, but I know others who have found them very helpful.

There are also support groups for families of people with mental illness, including depression. They are usually listed in newspapers' Community Events sections, and information can be obtained from family physicians and hospitals. If there isn't a local group, and we have the energy, we can start one for ourselves.

As a result of being part of a support group, I learned about clinical (or endogenous) depression, and realized it could be the reason I have fibromyalgia (the disease of chronic pain and extreme chronic fatigue). I was then able to confirm this with my family doctor and psychiatrist.

Psychotherapy

I have already acknowledged the help I have received from my psychiatrist. Several years ago, I received help from a psychologist. Going to the psychiatrist helped me to learn more about the

illnesses my mother had, as she has more specialized medical training than a psychologist. Both
psychology and psychiatry have caring, empathetic
professionals. There are also some that may not
provide the best kind of help. Finding the right
therapist may take some time.

One form of therapy that is gaining recognition and
some popularity is called Cognitive Behaviour
Therapy. In discussions with my psychiatrist for this
book, I learned that this is gaining in popularity for
its "pop psychology" approach, using the power of
positive thinking. This therapy takes the approach
that we all replay "tapes" in our head of previous
events and conversations, and those "tapes" need
to be reprogrammed. It is sometimes touted as
short term compared to other forms of psychotherapy.

While remaining positive and thinking of a brighter
future is important, sometimes problems are more
complex, and as much as everyone would like the
therapy to be brief, there are times when a longer
term of therapy is needed.

Sometimes you *do* have to replay those 'negative
tapes' and do the hard work in order to really let go
of the past, which is important if you want to have a
healthy future.

There are a number of other therapies that I have
found very helpful. These are outlined in the book,
The Complete Book of Natural Pain Relief, by
Richard Thomas and Peter Albright, M.D., who
acted as Thomas' consultant.

Psychological Therapies

This group of therapies includes self-hypnosis, relaxation therapies, meditation, autogenic training, and biofeedback. These are therapies based on mental and emotional exercises that produce physical effects by processes increasingly understood by conventional medicine and science."[iv]

All of these therapies are good for self-help, once some training has been obtained from a health professional. However, that professional should be carefully chosen, as their skills may vary.

Self-hypnosis is a form of meditation, similar to Cognitive Behaviour Therapy. Affirmations are repeated, usually as the breathing slows, at a steady pace. Books, videotapes and audiotapes can be helpful when practicing self-hypnosis.

Relaxation therapies are also useful. While this might seem like a bit of a contradiction, one of the best ways to relax is to exercise, and the faster you move, the better. One of my favourite forms of exercise is swimming. Just moving through the water is calming--I find I can literally stop thinking about the outside world, and any problems that might be plaguing me, for at least the time I am in the water, because I concentrate on the activity. I've heard that people who run, play tennis, or ride bicycles have similar positive experiences.

If physical exercise is not possible, because of pain or a depressed mood that has zapped all energy, there are alternatives:

The most effective relaxation therapies that do not involve physical effort are visualization, meditation, and biofeedback. All three involve totally relaxing the body totally by making a conscious mental effort. They can be done quite quickly with the right instruction and practice.....Relaxation therapies are effective for aches and pains due to headaches, migraines, depression, back strain, breathing problems, asthma, angina, circulation problems, high blood pressure, stomachache, irritable bowel syndrome, nerve pain, eczema, psoriasis, sexual problems, and cancer.[v]

In some of the personal stories shared in this book, anxiety and panic attacks are mentioned as a symptom of the depression many women suffered. Breathing problems, asthma, angina, headaches, migraines, stomachaches, and irritable bowel syndrome are often associated with these anxiety and panic attacks, according to some doctors.

I found it helpful to have instruction from a psychologist to learn some methods of self- hypnosis and meditation. Visualizing physical pains as large balls of wool that gradually unravel as they go down a flight of stairs, (as I lay or sit very quietly counting backwards from 20) is particularly effective. I sometimes visualize that I can put anger and hurt into a large container and throw it into the lake. These may seem simplistic, but they work for me. I have heard that writing your problem on a piece of paper and then burning it in a fireplace can be useful. I find looking at a fire is a calm and peaceful activity, as is sitting beside a calm lake or river.

Resting the mind provides a greater capacity for healing. Meditation has been described as active concentration. There are a number of techniques for meditation. Some of them, such as transcendental meditation (TM) are quite famous, and popular. Many of today's celebrities including Alanis

Morissette and Madonna have gone to India to learn more about these meditative techniques, and the Eastern religions on which they are based. I hate to break anyone's illusions, but this is not a recent trend. The Beatles visited India in the 60s and much of the Eastern religion influences showed up in *their* music.

Meditation takes practice. The theory is that once the mind is relaxed, the body will become relaxed, enabling healing. I know there have been many times, (especially during the writing of this book), that I had difficulty relaxing, or getting to sleep because my mind was still racing! Meditating helped to relax me enough to fall asleep. I probably should do it more often than I do, but what I take comfort from is the fact that I have learned how to do this, and it has helped. I often light candles when I meditate.

Sitting around a single flame can awaken in us the primordial instincts of the cave dweller, when it was the fire that kept the wild animals at bay, and when it was the only source of light and heat.
It evokes feelings of comradeship, friendship, and security......
Meditate on the light of a candle flame. Then with love, kindle a small light in your heart.[vi]

Autogenic training is related to meditation, self-hypnosis, and yoga. With this type of training, you become aware of your breathing, your heartbeat, and your movements, or lack of them.

Creative arts therapies involving art, sand play, dance, music, and drama are effective ways of expressing feelings--both positive and negative. Quite often, it is the fact of not being able to express negative feelings that can lead to depression, which can lead to more serious problems of addiction.

Therapies such as reflexology, acupressure, reiki, and therapeutic touch are also discussed in the book about natural forms of pain relief. These are grouped as "Subtle Energy Therapies". I have had some success with these but have not used them often. Others have had more success.

Bridget's Story:

I believe that I have had periods of depression throughout my life, but I did not know how to identify them. It was not until I could not live a useful life that I began to accept that I needed help with this problem.

Once you have been depressed, and have identified it as such, you become aware of what to look out for...I still have one or two days of the month when I panic, thinking that I am becoming depressed again. It is not a place that I want to return. I think I could say that I have depressive periods, but not full blown depression. It is a constant battle with myself.

I believe that I had a post-partum depression after my first child was born. I felt post-partum for two years! ...I lost my identity when I became a mother. I no longer knew who I was. My daughter was a determined child (and still is) ...I had a lot of anxiety. There were real reasons for this sometimes, but even if there was no reason, I had an overwhelming sense of doom. It is a terrible feeling.....My life was never what I wanted it to be.. Temper tantrums, rages, crying, sadness, fatigue, overeating, headaches, moodiness, trouble with staying asleep.

My daughter ran away from home when she was 16. The years of stress preceding that event led to a depression from which I was unable to extricate myself. After she returned home, I could not understand why I did not feel better.

I had spent about two years trying naturopathic remedies, and have a cupboard full of herbs and vitamins that did not help.

My doctor had wanted to put me on an antidepressant, but I did not want to take medication. One night I sat up crying all night because my son had skipped school once again. I was considering which bridge to jump off. That was when I knew that I had to take the plunge and go on antidepressants. I had thought of suicide before, but I had never actually come up with a plan. I was scaring myself!!! I finally became my own best friend, and took myself to the doctor! I became acquainted with "the sin of pride." I was too prideful to want to take medication (though I would not think less of someone else if they did). The winter is the worst for me. I used a full spectrum light last winter. That seems to help. During the time that I took medication, I learned many other ways to handle stress. I explored deep breathing and meditation. I also took steps to establish some other identity besides "mother". I went to university to pursue a BA in Sociology. (I have been a RN since 1972). I became a volunteer for a mental health agency. I became involved with work in my church. I learned Therapeutic Touch.

I have gone through various periods of time when I drank too much. I do not drink too much now. I want to live a more authentic lifestyle. I also know that I am an emotional eater and have gained far too much weight over the years. My alcohol cravings are basically sugar cravings, I think. I have substituted bags of M & Ms for the rum and cokes. My body did not like that any better than the alcohol! I also eat a lot better now. I listen to my body... sometimes it whispers, and sometimes it shouts! It will always be a struggle.

I smoked until I was 25 when I got pregnant with my first child. I never started again. I am glad that this is one way of self-medicating that I got control of early.

My mother did not drink alcohol, nor was she depressed as far as I know. She was very self-righteous about alcohol. My father drank a lot, and I now believe that he had periods of depression... or perhaps a constant state of depression. My mother and dad were hit by a drunk driver in 1984.

My dad died following the accident. He was not drinking at the time, but the irony of that accident haunts me. He was a good man who drank. Love the person, hate the behaviour. I only recognized the similarity in my behaviour after he was dead - the rage, the sullen silence. Perhaps he felt trapped. I feel that way often.

I now prefer to lose myself in books, studies, writing and other ways of challenging my mind. Alcohol interferes with doing those things. I now prefer to practice relaxation techniques, walk the Labyrinth, do Therapeutic Touch, pray and explore other ways of bringing healing to others and myself. I think my use of alcohol was in part a rebellion against who I really am. I rebelled against being such a good girl, I wanted to be a bit of a brazen woman. I still enjoy altered states of consciousness, but prefer to acquire them through use of the Labyrinth or other meditative techniques rather than alcohol.

My daughter and my son both exhibit symptoms of depression. Both use alcohol, though I can not tell you if it is to excess, as they do not drink very much in my presence. I have told them that they have a familial tendency toward alcoholism (on both sides of the family), and that they should be aware of that. They both smoke cigarettes and my son smokes pot.....

Nobody's life is perfect, but we have to live our own lives, so each person's problems are the biggest for them. I do get depressed over things in my life that I can not change. I get frustrated and feel trapped. I weigh the pros and cons and make my decisions. I constantly try to explore and learn new things so that I am stimulated and always feel a forward thrust. When I feel stagnant I flounder and plunge. I can't afford to allow myself the luxury of wallowing in self-pity. I choose to help others who are in need. Two tools that I use are also tools that give back to me and aid in my own healing. I facilitate labyrinth walks, but I also benefit by walking myself. When I give Therapeutic Touch treatments, I receive benefits for myself. These are two ways that in giving I, too, receive.

My Christian faith is very important to me. I have a purpose and I can not fulfil it if I linger in depression.

My faith fills me with hope for the future and with support and encouragement for my work. It is an essential part of my being. When I hear "hope based research" I think of people sharing stories that can make them feel like they are not alone, that they can see that change is possible.

Bridget recognizes that no one's life is perfect, and anyone can become depressed. She says there is a time to let go of the "sin of pride" and get help. It took a long time and trying different therapies for Bridget to decide what would work for her. She also turned to her faith for help, and found it. She also seems to have come to the realization that "she has a purpose". We all do. Sometimes that purpose gets lost in our sea of depression, or drowned in alcohol.

The healing arts of reiki and therapeutic touch might seem similar to the "hands-on" faith healing used by some evangelists. If given by a qualified practitioner, these therapies are very helpful. Some people do not believe that these really work, or if they do work, it is because the person *wants* them to work, and convinces themselves that these therapies are useful. (These people may be among those who do not believe that depression is a serious illness.) There will always be skeptics, and we cannot listen to them. We have to trust in our own abilities to heal.

Therapeutic Touch (TT) is often done by registered nurses with special training. It is based on the theory of a transfer of energy from the toucher to the person being touched and the so-called negative energy, or pain, being pulled from the patient. Most times, the TT practitioner does not touch the person they are healing.

Reiki (pronounced "ray-kee", meaning universal life force) is another variation of a "hands-on" art that has become more popular lately, although its roots can be traced back more than 100 years, and is based on ancient Tibetan Bhuddist methods. It involves a transfer of restorative energies from one person to another.

These practices have been used successfully with people who have panic attacks and anxiety. They are also helpful for headaches, migraines, back pain, asthma, infections, and cancer.

I have discussed these in detail because I thought they might not be as well known [as other types of therapies described later]. I can personally vouch for the success in treating some of the symptoms of my depression, including headaches, migraines, neck and back pain, and insomnia using the psychological and subtle energy therapies.

Almost all of these therapies are complemented by aromatherapy, using oils distilled from plants considered to have health properties. These include lavender, for sleep and relaxation, and juniper berry for energy. (There are too many to list here, but a trip to your library or health food store will help you learn more about them. Stores such as The Body Shop also carry aromatherapy products.) A note of caution--essential oils can be harmful if ingested, and some should not be used by very young women, pregnant women or women who are breast-feeding. Someone who is trained in the use of aromatherapy products (e.g. candles) should be consulted.

Homeopathic treatments, which are usually from plants or minerals, can also bring relief for many ailments often treated with conventional medicine. However, this is not an area for self-medicating, even though these remedies are available over the counter. Consultation with a qualified homeopath is recommended.

Movement therapies

Movement therapies such as yoga and tai chi are gaining popularity for relaxing the mind, as well as relaxing and stretching the body. One of the symptoms of my depression is fibromyalgia, characterized by chronic pain and extreme fatigue. Doing some yoga at least once a week is very helpful to keeping those muscles healthy. I have taken yoga classes, and have a couple of books for use at home. I also have videotape so I can follow a qualified teacher. I've tried tai chi, but found the movements too slow. Others enjoy that slower pace.

Participating in an exercise class, or going out for a walk once in a while is probably better than always doing exercises by yourself at home.
Being in a social situation is as healthy for our minds as the exercise is for our bodies. It may also lead to developing friendships that then become part of a strong support network needed for optimum health. Besides, I get bored with only myself for company all the time, don't you?

While the above therapies can be done at home, once you've had some training, there are others that should **only be done by a fully qualified**

professional all the time. These include acupuncture, chiropractic care, massage therapy, osteopathy, (including cranial osteopathy), and the psychotherapy and hypnotherapy mentioned earlier. I can attest to the successful treatments by my chiropractor and massage therapist for treating the aches and fatigue associated with the fibromyalgia. (I have not tried the others).

The manipulation I receive of my neck and spine from the chiropractor is sometimes very gentle. Other times it is more pronounced. I always feel relief. I have seen, through computer-generated scans, that there continues to be improvement in the alignment of my spinal column. I can feel there is more energy flowing through.

Chiropractic is founded upon a single, basic premise: all living things have an inborn or innate wisdom or healing ability, which constantly works to maintain us in health, and heal us if we are injured or diseased....The goal of chiropractic care is the correction of the vertebral subluxation (a misaligned vertebra causing interference with nerve messages between your brain and your body; a spinal abnormality that interferes with your nerves.) It [the subluxation] can create dis-ease: lowered resistance to disease, pain, imbalance, fatigue, and can pave the way for ill health...Doctors of chiropractic specialize in locating, analyzing, and correcting vertebral subluxations[vii]

Massage therapy has also worked for me to alleviate pain and improve my mood.

While having a friend or family member give you a gentle massage is very relaxing, and therefore healing, true massage therapy should only be done by a Registered Massage Therapist (RMT) with that specialized training and knowledge of the body's nervous and lymphatic systems.

The effectiveness of massage lies in stimulating blood flow, relaxing nerves and muscles, and in the psychological benefits of feeling "cared for". The variations available are enormous, from the relatively strong techniques used in Swedish massage to methods so gentle that they hardly seem like massage at all, and have more in common with the "soft-tissue" manipulation used by some osteopaths or "hands-on" healers.[viii]

It took me a while to find a massage therapist and chiropractor with whom I was comfortable. I know there are some who have had little or no relief from these treatments, so research and being willing to be a "lab rat" to see if these therapies are appropriate and helpful for us is necessary.

It can be tiresome, and somewhat depressing to have to do all of this work. That's why I don't do all of it, at least not all at once! If I did, I wouldn't have had time to do anything else. I'd always be running to one health care professional or another. I also believe that while these people are excellent resources for good health, and help me to stay healthy, ultimately the person in charge of my health is me. I decide to seek help, as I need it.

My mother, (and many of the mothers of the other women whose stories are in the book) decided *not* to get the help they might have needed. In almost all cases, they denied they had a problem, and they didn't want to talk about their health. Perhaps they all had the "sin of pride". People didn't talk about their health problems with their families, let alone on national television and in magazines, as is the case today. (Although there are times when some of those people should not be quite so forthcoming!) It helps to share a problem, and it helps to know you are not alone.

Although it is known that genetics play a significant role in depression and alcoholism, the specific genes have not yet been isolated. Therefore, it is not as easy to screen for these illnesses as it is for some others, e.g. cancer. There is research being done on a new screening tool to predict the recurrence of depression at the CAMH. There is hope. Depression <u>can</u> come to an end, as demonstrated in the following story by Rosie Rosenzweig, a resident scholar at Brandeis University in Massachusetts.

I remember exactly when it started, and exactly how it ended. I remember the crisis that resulted, its spastic undoing or denouement, and the conversation that began the process back to full engagement. The story has been writing itself for about thirty years.

I had just arrived at a point in my life when the plan to write was put into a schedule. My two older children were both in school, so that I went to the typewriter, wherever it was located be it the kitchen, our bedroom, or the living room, and wrote poetry. The joy of reworking words to frame experience was such a fine way to live-- or so I thought-- until three deaths changed my life.

First my older sister, then my older brother, and then, my father, died within a short time after the birth of my youngest child. I took her with me to the town where my father died. Although she stayed with a sitter during the burial, I can still hear the sounds I heard that day as I entered the cemetery to witness the lowering of my father's casket --that of my baby crying and my breaking into sobs uncontrollably. It took years to keep in my memory the dates of the deaths: 1968, 1969, and 1970.

My husband had various suggestions for curing my depression, which included visits to the Esalen Institute and involvement in various encounter groups, and I was driven to repair myself. Damage to our marriage ensued, and the depression with intense anxiety became stronger.

I approached suicide like a warrior and got very close, but somehow this plunged me into long-term therapy with a psychiatrist that began to pull me out of the black hole.
I began to work full-time in 1977 in education and then in the business world, and a sense of self-worth resumed with great intensity. I became involved with the many observances of my Judaism and my many co-religionists. My marriage repaired, but another death, my mother's in 1990, and a layoff, the first of the computer industry's economic roller coaster, turned me downward once again.

Another death, that of my brother-in-law, opened another door to healing. My ailing mother-in-law, who had helped me immensely during my lifetime, pleaded with me to help her daughter. So I went and cared for her, and for her family during the burial and the mourning period. I managed her kitchen and meals, and thereafter when she came to Boston continued to look after her. I believe this type of giving allows one to come out of oneself and see the larger world, to see that giving is expansive, and to understand that it is an antidote to depression.

Afterwards I began a new career as a Hebrew schoolteacher, writer, and workshop facilitator. I wrote two books and several articles, which were presented in various venues. I also began an intensive study and practice of different forms of meditation. Now I am a scholar in a Women's' Studies Program, publishing, lecturing, and planning a meditation society for my academic community. I have numerous resources in these circles, and in my spiritual community. Perhaps I will write about this more, and offer help to others, as I continue on my journey to recovery.[ix]

Rosenzweig has clearly come through very difficult times. She and Bridget feel that by helping and teaching others, they have helped themselves. These women have also come to accept themselves, as they are, sad past and all.

Mora, whose story is part of the second chapter, has learned from her sad past. She is headed towards a brighter future.

I have suffered from periods of depression since adolescence. I know I had suicidal thoughts, but I thought that most teenagers did, so I did not think this unusual or abnormal.

I think a lot of it was how I felt about growing up female, and how I thought this really sucked (pardon my poor English). ...I thought the world was against girls and women.

My mother was in her late 30s and my father in his 40s when I was born. This generation gap made it nearly impossible for them to relate to the events unfolding in my life. I think all of my mother's anxiety and depression manifests in her children.... I often find it hard to be around her because I find her life to be so depressing that I can barely stand it without losing it myself.....She will not seek help, or make any changes in her life.....She continues to drink quite a lot, but always chastises those who she thinks drink too much...My symptoms started to make sense after my older sisters told me about my mother's depression, which started when I was born, and their own depression.

....Sometimes I wonder if there is anyone who is <u>not</u> depressed. Living in Los Angeles when I was in my late 20s, I experienced my worst depression. I hated living in that city. I did a lot of partying, mostly drinking....Interestingly, coming out as a lesbian during that time did not add to my depression. If anything, it helped relieve it.... It was at this time that I was first <u>diagnosed</u> with depression. I went to a psychiatrist, and we tried several different types of anti-depressants. I finally started to get some relief from the depression, and while driving my car one day, I thought to myself, "wow, <u>this</u> is what it feels like to be happy." The world felt like a better place, and my optimism was restored.

However, that drug gave my dizzy spells, and I had to stop taking it. I moved away from Los Angeles, and I haven't taken any anti- depressants since then. I still experience bouts of depression, but nothing as severe as during that time…. I know what it feels like now, and I have a huge fear of, falling into it again. It is a big, black, heavy hole that feels impossible to climb out of. I know it's hard to treat depression on your own, but I now feel like I can take some preventative measures…. I have done this through building social support networks, eating better and physical activity. It is still extremely difficult. I am motivated by my extreme dislike of medication. When I get down now, I tell myself that it will pass, that it is just circumstance. But I know what depression feels like, and most of the time; I can work through it, and feel better.

I enjoy reading all types of writing. I am fond of inspirational books, especially ones written with a sense of humour. This is from the book <u>Succulent Wild Woman</u> by Sark. She calls this piece "Radical Self-Acceptance" It is the perfect antithesis for this chapter, and made me laugh so hard, I cried.

Do not stand naked in front of your mirror and accept what you see,
Wear large pajamas and stay in bed all day.
Buy or borrow self-improvement books, but don't read them.
Stack them around your bedroom and use them as places to rest bowls of cookies.
Watch exercise shows on television, but don't do the exercises. Practice believing that the benefit lies in imagining yourself doing the exercises.
Don't power walk. Saunter slowly in the sun, eating chocolate, and carry a blanket so you can take a nap.
….Simply luxuriate in where you are right now. Read this. Breathe. Adopt this philosophy. Of course you might begin new exercise plans, meditate more often, blah, blah, blah. But where are you right now?[x]

If we are not where we want to be, we will get there.

Endnotes:

[i] Lyrics from "You Learn" by Alanis Morissette, from Jagged Little Pill , Copyright Alanis Morrisette, All Rights Reserved(1995)

[ii] "Just For Today", Al-Anon Family Groups, reprinted, 1997, Copyright, Al-Anon Family Groups, All Rights Reserved

[iii] Ibid

[iv] Thomas, Richard, with Albright, Peter, M.D. (Consultant) The Complete Book of Natural Pain Relief, Firefly Books, Quarto Publishing, 1998, p. 136

[v] Ibid, p. 137

[vi] Smith, Pam, Smith, Gordon, Meditation, A Treasury of Technique, C.W.Daniel Company, 1989

[vii] Koren, Tedd, D.C., "The Chiropractic Source", Koren Publications, copyright, 1997, All rights reserved

[viii] Thomas, Richard with Albright, Peter, M.D. The Complete Book of Natural Pain Relief, Firefly Books, 1998, p. 128

[ix] Rosenzweig, R., Untitled, from a soon to be published work, All rights reserved 2001.

[x] Sark, Wild Succulent Woman, Fireside Books, Simon&Schuster,1997, p. 112

Research Information

This is a little background on how this book came to be. It probably should have been called the "Foreword" and been at the front of the book, but I wanted you to read the book first. I hope you have, and not jumped right to this page.

This book has been in my head for about three years--maybe longer. As I watched my mother's health deteriorate, I became more determined to learn from what I observed. I became even more determined (than I already was) to live a healthier life.

In my journals, I was writing about her poor health, and the sadness and anger I felt about the fact that she was not taking better care of herself. At the same time, I was writing about what a vibrant person she had been, and how much I had learned from her. (I knew, even though doctors had not said anything concrete, that my mother was not going to live a long, healthy life. She started having more serious health problems at the age of 65 and died when she was 68)

That writing developed into an academic paper I presented at an international conference on Mothers and Education held in 1999 sponsored by the Association for Research on Mothering (ARM). In writing that paper, I learned to love the process of research. I also knew I wanted to keep writing about my mother.

I had already started writing about mothers and health, and what we learn from that. My mother was an alcoholic, and she was depressed.
I needed to put my experience into a larger context. I also needed to fully grieve her death. Writing this has been very cathartic. I could not have written the book before her death, but I have felt her guiding me. I think she would be proud of me for writing with such honesty. She taught my sister and me to always be honest, even if we couldn't always be kind.

In 2001, the ARM conference theme was to be "Mothering, Literature, the Arts and Popular Culture". I submitted an abstract to the conference committee about a paper discussing alcohol and drugs in popular culture, and the effect that might have on our behaviour. That abstract was accepted. I realized that there was a much longer story to be told. The paper became a chapter of the book, and my presentation would include other information from the book.

I wanted to make this "hope-based research". I wasn't just describing the woes of these illnesses, and I didn't want this to be just my story. The focus of the book was to look at the patterns of depression and alcoholism in mothers and daughters, and learn how to break those patterns. I wanted to show that there was hope for a healthier future. I also wanted to bring some humour to the piece, to offset the serious nature of the subject matter.

Then the hard work of the research and writing began. I am a freelance writer and researcher, not connected with a university or any other institution, but I wanted to use good research methods. I contacted the Research Services office at Queen's University in Kingston, Ontario, Canada, and followed guidelines received from that office to construct a letter of information and consent form for anyone whose stories would be used in the book.

I needed to find out if I was alone in my experiences with a depressed and alcoholic mother. I suspected I was not, but was not sure how to proceed. With the help of the Administrative Co-ordinator at ARM, Cheryl Dobinson, I sent out an email asking if there were ARM members who would like to share their stories of living in similar circumstances to mine. The response was immediate, and I knew I had struck a chord. I had the personal stories for my book.

I developed a list of questions. (See Appendix). Participants were free to decline answers to any questions, or discuss any areas with which they were not comfortable. Some of the women answered each question, others used the questions as a guideline to tell their story. Participation was completely voluntary, and could have been withdrawn at any time. There was no compensation for participation.

Depression and alcoholism are not "cheery subjects". Thinking and writing about them was hard for me, as I am sure it was difficult for the other women. I was the only one to see the full stories. I have used all of the stories I received, in an edited form My sister and my husband, who were my editors, only saw my edited versions of the personal stories. . Each woman was sent the edited version of her story for approval before the manuscript was sent to the publisher.

The stories had to be put into context. I visited libraries and bookstores to continue my research. My reading was selective, but covered all of the aspects I wanted to touch on in this book.

Coming up with the title was a process of brainstorming with the women who were sharing their stories, my family, and the woman who was going to design the cover. "Breaking Patterns" was actually the working title of the book, until I found another book called "Breaking Patterns of Depression". Then I focused on learning from our mothers' depression and alcoholism. That became the subtitle. Still needing a main title, we focused on the "hope" aspect of the book. I remembered a Paul McCartney song "Hope of Deliverance", with the line, "hope of deliverance from the darkness that surrounds us." (I actually thought it was called "Hope of Eternity", and that was going to be the title). After more thought, it seemed important to concentrate on the hope and the learning aspect. I had decided that I also wanted the title to reflect the humour. Hence, the final title: **With Humour and Hope**: *Learning from Our Mothers' Depression and Alcoholism*. It's still a bit of a mouthful, but accurately describes the subject matter.

The process of this research and writing has been good for me for many reasons. I hope it brings equally good things to those who read it.

What it will be like
I don't know
When it will be light
I don't know
We live in hope of deliverance
From the darkness that surrounds us.[i]

[i] Lyrics from, "Hope of Deliverance" from "Off The Wall"
Copyright Paul McCartney, MPL Music, 1992, All Rights Reserved

Appendix

Questions sent to participants:

With Humour and Hope: *Learning from Our Mothers' Depression and Alcoholism*

Questions for participants:
Feel free to leave out any questions you find objection-able, or those making you uncomfortable. These questions are only a guideline. You may answer them directly, or use them in the telling of your story.

ABOUT YOU:

Have you ever suffered from periods of depression?

Do you still have depressive periods?

How do you, or did you recognize these periods? (What

are or were the symptoms?)

Did a physician diagnose this?

How has the depression been treated?

(check all that apply):

　　　　Medication (anti-depressants, e.g. Valium,

　　　　Adavan)

　　　　Self-"treatment" (alcohol, food, smoking, etc.)

Therapy (either in a group or individual)

Alternative therapies (e.g. meditation, yoga,

herbal treatments/vitamins, massage,

chiropractic, etc)

ABOUT YOUR MOTHER :

Has your mother had periods of depression?

Does she still have depressive periods?

Was there one event that triggered the depression, or

was it a number of small things?

What were the symptoms of the depression?

Did she realize herself that she was experiencing

depression, or was it understood more in hindsight?

Was it her that recognized the depression, or was it

another family member or friend?

Did a physician ever diagnose the depression?

How was the depression treated? (see the above list)

Are you aware of any pre-dispositions you might have to

addictive behaviours ?(i.e. alcohol or substance abuse; addiction to medication, even those prescribed by a physician?, over or under-eating, etc.)

Is there anything you are doing to "break the pattern" of addictive and depressive behaviour you may have "inherited"? (e.g. therapy; changing your diet; exercising more; changing jobs, etc.)

YOUR CHILDREN (any age--even adult children)

Have you seen any addictive or depressive behaviour in your children?

What steps are you taking to teach your children about these "legacies" from you and/or your mother?

When you hear the terms "hope-based research", or "hope for breaking patterns of depression and alcoholism", what comes to your mind?

Is there anything else you would like to add from your own, or your family's history with either depression or alcoholism?

Epilogue

As I was finishing the work on the book, the terrorist attacks on the United States shook the world. Talk about depressing!

There will be an increased need for grief counseling and therapy to deal with this terrible tragedy. Anyone who has a predisposition to the illnesses of depression or alcoholism will have an increased risk of becoming ill.

Having this book to finish gave me a much-needed focus. This is when staying busy really does help to keep your mind off of depressing thoughts. Taking the time to reflect on the events of the week, and pray for those who lost their lives, their families, and those who are in any way affected by this tragedy was also important to maintaining my own health and sense of well-being.

Tragic events do happen, although there has been nothing on this scale for many, many years. How we react to, and deal with the tragedy, is very individual. Coming together with others helps us to deal with that grief. Perhaps reading spiritual or other inspirational material comforts us.

It is also important to remember that life does, and should go on, and there can be humour even in the face of the most horrific events. It is important to continue to laugh. That laughter is part of our hope for the future.

Bibliography

This is a selective bibliography, and not a complete list of books, publications, and periodical literature dealing with depression and alcoholism. These are books I used as reference, and others I found. I hope you find this list helpful.

Ackerman, Robert J., <u>Perfect Daughters - Adult Daughters of Alcoholics</u>, Health Communications, Inc., 1989

Casey, Nell, <u>Unholy Ghost: Writers on Depression</u>, HarperCollins, 2001

DePaulo, Raymond J. Jr., M.D., and Ablow, Keith Russell, M.D., <u>How to Cope With Depression - A Complete Guide for You and Your Family,</u> McGraw-Hill Publishing Company, 1989

Douglas, Ann, <u>The Incredible Shrinking Woman: The Girlfriend's Guide to Losing Weight</u>, Prentice Hall Canada, 2000

Duke, Patty, and Turan, Kenneth, <u>Call Me Anna</u>, Bantam Books, 1987

Forward, Susan, <u>Toxic Parents: Overcoming their Hurtful Legacy and Reclaiming Your Life</u>, Bantam, 1989

Jung, John, <u>Psychology of Alcohol and Other Drugs--A Research Perspective</u>, Sage Publications, 2000

Klein, Donald F., M.D., and Wender, Paul H., M.D. <u>Understanding Depression - A complete Guide to its Diagnosis and Treatment</u>, Oxford University Press, 1993

Koren, Tedd, "The Chiropractic Source": pamphlet series, Koren Publications, 1997

Northrup, Christiane, M.D., <u>The Wisdom of Menopause</u>, Bantam Books, 2001

Papolos, Demitri, M.D., and Papolos, Janice, <u>Overcoming Depression</u> HarperCollins, 1997

Raskin, Valerie Davis, <u>When Words Are Not Enough, The Women's Prescription for Depression and Anxiety,</u> Broadway Books, 1997

"Rosie" September 2001, volume 128, number 11 Published Monthly by Gruner + Jahr USA Publishing

SARK, <u>Succulent Wild Woman</u>, Simon and Schuster, 1997

Shimberg, Elaine Fantle, <u>Depression: What Families Should Know</u>, Ballantine Books (division of Random House), 1991

Smith, Pam, Smith, Gordon, <u>MEDITATION: A Treasury of Technique</u>, C.W. Daniel Company, 1989

Susann, Jacqueline, <u>Valley of The Dolls</u>, Bantam, 1963

Thomas, Richard with Albright, Peter, M.D., <u>The Complete Book of Natural Pain Relief,</u> Firefly Books, 1998

Vellerman, Richard, and Orford, Jim, <u>Risk and Resilience - Adults Who Were the Children of Problem Drinkers</u>, Harwood Academic Publishers, 1999

Vista Hill Foundation, newsletter on Drug Abuse and Alcoholism, June 1995

Woititz, Janet Gerringer, Ed.D., <u>Adult Children of Alcoholics</u>,
Health Communications Inc., 1983

Whitfield, Charles L., <u>Healing the Child Within: Discovery and Recovery for Adult Children of Dysfunctional Families</u>, Health Communications Inc., 1987

"Women and Drinking", publication of the Addiction Research Foundation (Centre for Addiction and Mental Health), and AWARE (Action on Women's Addictions, Research and Education), Copyright 1996

"Women and Alcohol", publication of the Addiction Research Foundation (Centre for Addiction and Mental Health), and AWARE (Action on Women's Addictions, Research and Education), Copyright 1999

Yapko, Michael D., Ph.D., <u>Breaking the Patterns of Depression</u>, Doubleday, 1997

Resources

As with the bibliography, this is a selected list. I am sure there are resources I have not listed here. My apologies for any omissions. They are not deliberate. There are resources listed in some of the books listed in the bibliography. The organizations, agencies, and websites are listed in no particular order. I hope they are helpful.

A family physician is a good place to start. She or he can refer you to appropriate professionals and organizations in your community. Checking the phone book, or local Community Information directory is also a good idea. There are other mutual-help groups in communities. These include Narcotics Anonymous (NA) and Women for Sobriety (WFS). There may also be support groups for people suffering from depression in the area. The doctor or local health unit should have information about these.

The public library is also a valuable resource. Many of the books listed in the bibliography may be in the library, or can be ordered through Inter-Library Loan services. My librarian found many of the books on depression listed in the bibliography for me to use as research material.

Alcoholics Anonymous (www.alcoholics-anony-
mous.org), and its support groups for families
and friends, Al-Anon should be listed in the
local phone book, or local Community
Information Directory.

World Service Office for Al-Anon and Al-Ateen
1600 Corporate Landing Parkway
Virginia Beach, VA   23454-5617
U.S.A.
Phone: 757-563-1600; Fax: 757-563-1655

Association for Research on Mothering (ARM)
726 Atkinson
York University
4700 Keele Street
Toronto, ON   M3J 1P3
Phone: 416-736-2100; Fax: 905-775-1386
Email: arm@yorku.ca
Website: www.yorku.ca/crm

Canadian Association for Children of Alcoholics
Hospital for Sick Children
555 University Avenue, Room 5290
Toronto, ON
Canada
Phone: 416-813-5629; Fax: 416-813-5619

Centre for Addiction and Mental Health (CAMH)
33 Russell Street, Suite 4023, Toronto, Ontario
M5S 2S1
Canada
Tel. (416) 535-8501 ext 4484
24-hour Information line: (416) 595-6111

Ontario Toll-Free: 1-800-463-6273
Fax (416) 260-4125
www.camh.net

This is an "amalgamation" of the resources of
four (4) agencies:
Addiction Research Foundation
Clarke Institute of Pyschiatry
Donwood Institute
Queen Street Mental Heath Centre

There are two libraries, which are open to the
public. Please contact them [the CAMH] for further information. The CAMH also has a self-
help book called DrinkWise. It can be used on
your own at home to quit or cut down on your
drinking. The book may be ordered by calling
1-800-661-1111

Community Programs
80 Queen Street
Kingston, Ontario, Canada
(613) 546-4266

AWARE (Action on Women's Addictions--
Research and Education)
P.O. Box 86
Kingston, Ontario   K7L 4V6
Canada
613- 545-0117

Canadian College of Naturopathic Medicine
2300 Yonge Street, 18th Floor
P.O. Box 2431, Toronto,   ON M4P 1E4

Canada
Canadian Holistic Medical Association
42 Redpath Avenue
Toronto, ON   M4S 2J6
Canada

Canadian Natural Health Association
439 Wellington Street
Toronto, ON   M5V 2H7
Canada

National Depressive and Manic-Depressive
Association (NDMDA)
730 N. Franklin St., Suite 501
Chicago, IL 60610
800-826-3632 or 312-642-0049
www.ndmda.org

National Mental Health Association (NMHA)
1021 Prince St.
Alexandria, VA   22314
U.S.A.
800-969-NMHA
www.nmha.org

National Alliance for the Mentally Ill (NAMI)
Colonial Place Three
2107 Wilson Blvd., Suite 300
Arlington, VA   22201
U.S.A.
800-950-NAMI
www.nami.org

American Holistic Medicine Association
6278 Old McLean Village Drive
McLean, VA   22101

U.S.A.
National Center for Homeopathy
801 N. Fairfax Street, No. 306
Alexandria, VA   22314
U.S.A.

Office of Alternative Medicine
9000 Rockville Pike, Building 31
Room 5-B-38
Bethesda, MD   20892
U.S.A.

Australian Medical Faculty of Homeopathy
49 Cecil Street, Denistone East
NSW, Australia

Australian Traditional Medicine Society
27 Bank Street, Meadowbank
NSW, Australia

National Herbalists Association
Suite 305, BST House
3 Smail Street
Broadway NSW 2007
Australia

British Homeopathic Association
27A Devonshire Street
London   W1N 1RJ
U.K.

Council for Complementary and Alternative
Medicine
Suite D, Park House
206-208 Latimer Road
London   W10 1RJ

U.K.
Register of Complementary Practitioners
P.O. Box 194
London SE16 1QZ
U.K.

Other Websites:

The National Institutes of Health (NIH)
www.nih.gov

The Canadian Network for Mood and Anxiety
Treatments (CANMAT)
www.canmat.org

The Canadian Mood Disorders Association
website:
www3.sympatico.ca/mdamt

For information on health related surveys:
www.surveyresearchgroups.com

Contact Information

This journey to healthier future continues. If you'd like to share your story of learning from a family history with these or any other illnesses, please contact me.

I can be reached by e-mail:
cpeets@CaptionsCommunications.ca

or by regular mail:

Captions Communications
184 Second Avenue
Napanee, Ontario
K7R 2J2
CANADA

To order copies of this book for your friends or family, contact me at the above address.

Notes

Notes

ISBN 155212964-0

9 781552 129647